SPEECH

AND

SOCIAL

HUBER W. ELLINGSWORTH
University of Hawaii

THEODORE CLEVENGER, JR.
University of Texas

ACTION

a strategy of

oral communication

Prentice-Hall, Inc., Englewood Cliffs, New Jersey

SPEECH AND SOCIAL ACTION: A Strategy of Oral Communication
Huber W. Ellingsworth and Theodore Clevenger, Jr.

ACKNOWLEDGMENTS

No book is entirely the product of its immediate authors. In one way or another, every author must draw on the resources of some intellectual community. Where we have been able to trace specific ideas in this book to other published works, we have cited them in footnotes. We are also indebted to many colleagues and students for their influence on our treatment of topics discussed here, although these less direct influences are too numerous to mention individually.

Neither is a book produced without technical support. In particular, we are grateful to Mrs. Beth Ann Magasano for typing early drafts of most chapters, to Mrs. Kay Davenport for producing the final copy of the complete manuscript, and to Sally Wilson of Prentice-Hall for thoughtful editorial advice.

PN
4121
.E46

© 1967 by PRENTICE-HALL, INC.
Englewood Cliffs, New Jersey

Current printing (last digit).
10 9 8 7 6 5 4 3 2

Library of Congress Catalog Card Number: 67:18925
Printed in the United States of America.

Prentice-Hall International, Inc., *London*
Prentice-Hall of Australia, Pty. Ltd., *Sydney*
Prentice-Hall of Canada, Ltd., *Toronto*
Prentice-Hall of India Private Ltd., *New Delhi*
Prentice-Hall of Japan, Inc., *Tokyo*

CONTENTS

v

chapter 1

INTRODUCTION

The student of public speaking can find on the market dozens of books designed to aid him in improving his speaking effectiveness. Why have the authors of this book chosen to add another to the assortment? Because we have felt the need in teaching public speaking, persuasion, and speech strategy for a text that gives attention to the meaningful relation of speaker, speech, and audience, and that places these factors in a broad social context.

Traditionally, speech instruction heavily emphasizes speech preparation and delivery, with a limited concern for the social processes that the speech must affect and be affected by. A few books and articles suggest useful means of analyzing psychological and social factors in communication, but they are not very concerned with how a public speaker might utilize these insights.

But one may ask, if the social aspects of communication are so important to understanding the act of public speaking, why do we not simply use one of the many available books about communication, or for that matter sociology, for information and advice? The answer is that until very recently communication theorists and social scientists have virtually ignored public speaking as an instrument of either communication or social action. Consequently, one looks in vain to these sources for counsel on the specific issues that arise in preparing for, presenting, and evaluating the effects of speeches. Issues that have been studied intensively by social scientists are closely related to many concerns in public speaking; but these relations are not likely to

3

be seen clearly or in the correct light until one is familiar with the specific problems connected with the public speech.

Perhaps the distinction between a view which focuses on the speech itself and a communication-oriented view of the public speaking act can best be dramatized by the following sets of contrasting statements:

If the speaker's primary concern is with the speech itself, then he is likely to believe that:	*If the speaker's concern is with both the speech and its social context, then we are likely to believe that:*
1. A speech can be constructed so as to be correct or incorrect.	1. Speech construction must vary in terms of the social context and the psychological state of speaker and listener at the time of utterance.
2. The major responsibility for the success of a good speech lies with the listeners.	2. The major responsibility for the success of any speech lies with the speaker.
3. The speaker will be optimistic about the success of his efforts.	3. The speaker will have only a tentative expectation of success.
4. Most of the speaker's available time should go into construction of an effective speech.	4. The speaker's time and energy should be divided among the first speech, evaluation of feedback, and planning for additional speeches.
5. A good speech is likely to have the same meaning for speaker and listener.	5. Speaker and listener can never have the same meanings for a speech.
6. Systems for getting information about reactions to the speech (feedback) are not very important.	6. Feedback systems are essential.

7. After the speech, the speaker feels anxiety as to whether or not he gave a good speech.

8. Failure or unanticipated response to a speech is often accompanied by intense emotions in the speaker.

7. After the speech, the speaker feels anxiety as to whether or not he correctly predicted the response of his listeners and concern over what he should do next.

8. Failure or unanticipated response is often accompanied by a reasonable analysis of what happened.

Not only do the "speech-oriented" and the "communication" approaches lead to different assertions about speaking, but more importantly, they lead to different issues and questions. There are still many unanswered (and even unasked) questions both about speech preparation and delivery and about the speech in its social context. No one book can attempt to deal with more than a few of these, and the author must hope that he has the most important ones. In searching for the important issues, this book will draw from both the "speech" and the "communication" points of view, while largely ignoring the distinction between them. In short, the student should not anticipate in the following chapters a *mixture* of speech and communication concepts, but rather a *blend* of them. We shall find that more often than not the important questions about public speaking are neither clearly "speech" questions nor "communication" questions; rather they are questions that will concern an individual who plans to use public speaking as an instrument of social action, and that either the speech approach or the communication approach or (more often) both can help us to answer.

THE CONCEPT OF SOCIAL ACTION

If we are to adopt the viewpoint that the study of public speaking should be conducted in a broad dimension, then we are free to consider, not a single speech, but all the speeches and other factors that are directed to promote a particular social change. A look at our society will suggest that almost every speech makes the most sense when viewed as part of a larger message in an extended time dimension. The United Fund campaign, lectures in a college course, the President's speeches on foreign or domestic policy, a community safe-driving program, a political candidacy, are examples of this "larger-speech" idea. Furthermore, we can observe that some people are strongly affected by some of these messages, some actively reject them, and some remain indifferent. In the time dimension, some persons quickly adopt new ideas and practices, some do not change until after their neighbors have, and others seem never to change. Of course, not all changes in people are planned, or are the result of someone's intent. The rise in the divorce rate and the increase in lung cancer since 1900 are examples of unanticipated change. But a significant number of the continual changes in attitude, belief, and practice result in part from a planned program of social action. These efforts to change people by altering their store of information, their beliefs, and their outlook are carried on by persons whom we can label *change agents.* One of the ways in which a change agent can function is by making public speeches. He speaks because he wishes to affect his environment or his relationship to it in some way. If he is strongly committed to produce change, he may develop a program of social action that involves a variety of ways of presenting his messages over a period of time. Let us now examine the nature of this public speaker/change agent in more detail.

A LOOK AT THE CHANGE AGENT

As we have just noted, social action is initiated by individuals who have a commitment to produce change or to facilitate changes already underway. This commitment may be in the form of a role requirement; that is, the individual's responsibility as an employee, a student, a clergyman, an executive, a teacher, or a Democrat may require his participation. Or he may voluntarily seek to initiate or join in change. He may be angry at what he identifies as corruption in government or injustice in a court of law. He may be excited because a new product on the market is superior to competing products. He may develop personal enthusiasm for, or violent antipathy to, one candidate for office. In these and a great many other situations, the individual may find a commitment to action.

He may elect to be a change agent because he perceives an immediate reward for his activities. The salesman working on commission is moved to secure the adoption of his product because additional sales increase his pay. Persons who view their activities as serving others may see reward in helping individuals to improve their lot in life or to realize their potential.

A more complex goal is long-range reward. The agent of change may undertake an immediate program of social action because he believes that by doing so he will contribute to broader and more distant changes. The politician who shakes hands and serves on a charity committee appreciates that he will affect people in ways immediately favorable to him and that these smaller acts mays contribute to his goal of greater political responsibility. The successful teacher works for short-term changes in his students, the results of which he hopes will be rewarding to him (and them) in the long run. Of course, the typical agent of change will derive his commitment from a combination of these factors.

Once the individual commits himself to make a change or join in a change, he inevitably is faced with the responsibility of doing something about it. He may feel a high degree of responsibility for the undertaking, or he may not show much concern. The degree to which he exerts himself will almost certainly be related to why he originally made the commitment. If what he is doing is a routine role requirement, he probably will not exert maximum effort, nor will he reject the responsibility entirely. If he observes and interprets his environment in a way that disturbs him deeply, or if he sees a significant reward for his activities, his feeling of responsibility will be higher. In fulfilling this commitment, he will resort to a great deal of communication. If the press, radio, and television are available and are relevant to his situation, he will probably utilize them in an attempt to affect large numbers of persons. If he is to work face-to-face with others, he will wish to utilize group discussion and conferences as a means of affecting people and to secure their help in planning and carrying out social action. In all these situations he may find it expedient to utilize such audio-visual aids as posters, models, slides, motion pictures, and recordings. Most significantly for our purpose, he may choose to make speeches.

The information the speaker gives, and the appeals he makes for action, will alter the ways his respondents see the world around them. He must perceive himself and his role accurately in order to decide the nature and extent of communication in which he will engage. He must decide when to speak or when to keep silent or when to use other methods of social influence in achieving his goals. If he concludes that public speaking is a useful method to him, then the responsibility that he assumed as a change agent becomes his burden as a public speaker. If his motivation for speaking is high, he will make a heavy investment of time and energy as he prepares and delivers his speeches.

Our concern in this book will be with the individual who has made a commitment and accepted a high degree of responsibility.

SUMMARY

We have set forth in this introductory chapter the necessity for studying speech in the broadest environment possible. The organization of the book is an attempt to show the interaction of a number of variables, rather than a chain of specific acts to be performed by the speaker. The speaker has been described as an agent of change who also develops a commitment to change. After commitment he generally becomes a spokesman for his cause and assumes responsibility for bringing about change.

Assignment: Characteristics of Change Agents

Virtually everyone has among his acquaintances a number of persons (including himself) who can be described as change agents—persons who by their statements and behavior indicate that they have a commitment to introduce or facilitate change in one or more situations. Select one of these change agents for particular attention. You may need to conduct an interview or other appropriate means of gaining information. Prepare a paper or oral report which includes the following information:

1. What is the nature of the change for which the individual is working?
2. How intensely does the individual appear to have committed himself to the change?
3. How long has he been functioning in the change agent role?
4. What sort of communication (conversation, speeches, writing, mass media) does he engage in while working for change?

chapter 2

STRATEGY

IN ORAL

COMMUNICATION

The scientific concept of process is a difficult and often frustrating way of looking at the world. It cuts across many of the comfortable and logical models upon which much of Western science and philosophy were based prior to the Twentieth Century. The idea that "everything affects everything else all the time" seems to point toward chaos and confusion in human thought, rather than to progress. In operation, however, this idea has spurred on the search for total descriptions of events and for differences that make a difference. Theories of rhetoric in speaking and writing have been slow to assimilate process notions, partly because these theories were formulated during the pre-scientific era. The impact of modern science on rhetoric has been to produce a reaction rather than a union that seeks truth by all available means. Some rhetoricians have reemphasized important traditions of liberalism and humanity; scientific communicologists in turn have pursued their goals through the canons of experimentalism and have sometimes rejected rhetoricians as intuitive, uninformed conservatives. Like all reactionary conflicts, this position-taking has cut both sides off from an understanding of the other's needs. The scientist exists in order to confirm and expand the limits of knowledge; the rhetorician finds his justification in helping the public speaker with day-to-day problems in practical communication.

The scientist's map of knowledge about communication contains far more unexplored territory than areas of confirmed hypothesis; the rhetorician often teaches from propositions that are inadequate or obsolete. It now becomes the task of speech scholars and practitioners to draw these concerns toward one another. The reader of this or similar books, therefore, should not seek either a scientific treatise on communication or a manual of practical procedures. For the reasons mentioned in chapter 1, we do not believe that either will best serve the interests of the serious student of public speaking. This chapter will present what the writers regard as a meaningful alternative. The six-stage strategy provides a broad map of the territory; the communication model describes the elements which will affect the success of the strategy.

When military commanders talk about "strategy," they mean the over-all planning and direction of a campaign aimed at accomplishing a particular major objective. This idea involves arranging matters in the most advantageous way prior to the action and then committing the men and material to the plan. Changing conditions during the engagement may, of course, force continual readjustments in the tactics by which the strategy is being carried out, but the basic plan provides a starting point and a major design within which such readjustment takes place.

The public speaker who hopes to succeed probably will not think of himself as a military force, nor of his audience as the enemy. But from the military analogy he may use the concept of careful advance planning, accompanied by flexibility to alter his plans as the situation changes. The strategy of oral communication will probably include at least the following major aspects:

I. *The speaker will identify respondents whom he believes can act in the way he wants.* Society is, by definition, an interlocking complex of smaller social groups. For that reason it is seldom possible to tell with certainty whether we have located all of the groups who might contribute in some way to the success or failure of a particular change. The speaker, therefore, should plan to contact both "primary" and "secondary" audiences and allocate his energy and resources according to how important he perceives each to be. Primary audiences are those persons in a position to act with effect toward the goal the speaker desires. Secondary audiences are involved less directly, and in a supporting capacity. For example, in this era of the civil rights movement, there have been few rallies or demonstrations in the states of Maine, North Dakota, or Alaska. Persons in these states may have a strong intellectual commitment to racial equality, and their attitudes and beliefs contribute to a national climate of opinion; but the relative absence of racial minorities in these states means that little energy has been expended by civil rights advocates in trying to produce a change in belief and conduct there, because citizens of those states are secondary audiences for integration messages.

Primary audiences of citizens for increased state aid to schools are likely to be parent-teacher groups, education associations, and legislators. A candidate for student body president will speak primarily to audiences of students, rather than faculty members, though he may welcome faculty support at a secondary level. The accomplishment of a complex goal will often require the support of *several* primary and secondary audiences. For instance, establishing a graduate program at a state university involves participation by audiences of faculty members, trustees, legislators, and students, as well as the technical or professional groups whom the graduates will serve when they leave the university.

Secondary audiences usually are important because of their potential influence over members of some primary audience. Thus, the student candidate may welcome faculty support because it helps to create a favorable climate of opinion which will influence student voters, and the breakfast cereal manufacturer directs advertising to young children (who cannot buy cereal) because of their influence over parents (who can). Sometimes, however, a secondary audience is important not so much because of the positive influence it can exert upon a primary audience, but because of the negative influence it might exert if it

14

should be ignored. Indeed, to by-pass any of the groups who regard themselves as either primary or secondary candidates for the proposed change may result not only in lost support, but in active opposition. So a necessary step in developing a strategy of oral communication is to identify major audiences of both kinds and to make a priority of available resources to reach them.

II. *The speaker will inventory information about the attitudes, knowledge, beliefs, and actions of each audience of respondents relative to his objectives.* One of the bases which the speaker is likely to use in identifying primary and secondary audiences is their degree of actual or potential involvement with the pro-posed change. This involvement is expressed in the formal ob-jectives of organized groups, in programs of action, in commit-ment of human and material resources, in the frequency with which the proposed change has been talked about, and in the record of similar past actions. If his estimate of a group's posi-tion is that it favors his objectives, he may decide that rela-tively little energy will be required to convert that group's existing beliefs and attitudes to acceptance. If there is evidence of open hostility, he will need to determine whether he can get along without the support of the group. He may choose to ignore the hostile audiences; however he should keep in mind that there have been experiments indicating that hostility can be reduced by communication when people have previously in-dicated a negative attitude.[1]

III. *The speaker will review his own knowledge, attitudes, and beliefs about the matter to be discussed.* An important feature of any such review is what might be called "intrapersonal reality testing." The speaker should realize that if he possesses a high degree of commitment toward a certain objective, he is likely to overestimate the potency of his cause. Or his perception of

[1]See, for example, J. W. Thibaut and J. Coules, "The Role of Communication in the Reduction of Interpersonal Hostility," *Journal of Abnormal and Social Psy-chology*, XLVII (1952), 770–77.

events relative to the proposed objective may be distorted, so that he sees a particular happening as being more favorable to his purpose than it will ultimately prove to be. On the other hand, if the speaker perceives too great a discrepancy between his own commitment and that of his target audiences, he may fall victim to delusions of martyrdom. His forecast of the speaking situation may then feature an image of himself carrying on a hopeless yet noble struggle against massive ignorance, folly, or indifference. He may then underestimate the potency of his cause or see a particular happening as being less favorable to his purpose than it will ultimately prove to be. Both overconfidence and despair are equally nonproductive. A carefully explicit examination of his own knowledge, attitudes, and beliefs about the topic may help to avoid both extremes.

Moreover, a comparison of his own knowledge, attitudes, and beliefs with those he observes in or infers from his target audiences may suggest the need to modify his public position. The accomplishment of objectives for change can be defined in terms of the distance that the speaker and respondent must move toward one another before understanding and acceptance are achieved. The speaker may decide in his preliminary planning that he must take a public position closer to where the group appears to be than he really feels in order to establish and develop his leadership.

IV. *The speaker will formulate messages designed to facilitate the desired response.* The task of speech construction represents one of the most difficult and exacting parts of the communication process. To be effective, the speech must constitute a skillful presentation of ideas designed to lead the respondent toward the speaker's viewpoint. It must include factual information about the events under consideration and demonstrate how statements about these events can be fitted into the framework of the respondent's knowledge and beliefs. Following strategic analysis of the situation, the speaker may conclude that the speech must be broken up into smaller message units and presented as several speeches over a period of time, or tied in with other communication events that may be occurring.

V. *The speaker will present the speech or speeches to his intended audience.* In the process of deciding *what* will be said, the source makes some, but not all, of the necessary decisions about *how* the speech will be formulated into a presentation system that is likely to contribute to understanding and acceptance. Since the only link between himself and the respondent is sensory experience, no matter how sophisticated and complex his ideas may be the speaker will review the verbal and visual possibilities for encoding his speech. These possibilities will be determined by the nature, complexity, and length of the speech, by what presentation devices are available, and by the nature of the situation in which the speech will be presented. Generally speaking, he will develop speeches that have enough repetition, or redundancy, to assure easy understanding, and sufficient variety to maintain attention.

VI. *The speaker will employ an evaluation system to determine how well his immediate and long-range objectives are being achieved.* No matter how skillfully the situation has been analyzed and the message prepared and presented, the proof of success lies in the changed behavior of the respondents. Some of the information about how well a speaker is doing is available continuously during the time he is speaking. Most speakers have an intuitive feeling about how well they are accomplishing their purposes, but more formal measures are sometimes available. For example, certain speakers, such as teachers, use formal measuring devices called examinations to determine the degree of their success. Attitude measures have been used by some speakers to examine the amount of shift in attitude after communication takes place. Still other evidence is how frequently a speech or its ideas are mentioned in a period of time following the speech. A good evaluation system may include both formal and informal measures, which begin at the time of the speech and continue afterward while the proposed change is likely to be taking place. These data will form the basis for decisions about whether additional speeches are necessary to increase the success of the effort.

The amount and extent of change will need to be accounted for when the whole strategic process is repeated for another communication plan. Means of carrying out this strategy of communication will be developed in the remainder of the book. First, however, we will discuss an organized way of looking at the speech situation by means of a model.

COMMUNICATION MODELS

If we are to consider how a strategy of speech and social action is to be implemented, we need a sufficiently detailed "map" of the territory to be investigated. The approach of most communication theorists has been to develop a visualization or model of communication. Usually this model attempts to discover and identify the major elements in the situation and to describe how the elements interact and affect one another. Because rigorous investigation of ingredients in the communication situation is relatively new, there is little general agreement as to how communication variables and their interaction should be specified; therefore, any communication model is more accurately described as speculative than descriptive. Another limitation on trying to make such pictures or descriptions is that communication is by definition a dynamic, ongoing process, whereas a model is static and inflexible.

Despite the fact that no one is entirely sure what should go into a communication model, and regardless of the inadequacies of words or pictures to convey the process, a number of models are available which help to stimulate and organize our thinking about communication.

Verbal Models

One of the oldest and best-known verbal models is found in Aristotle's *Rhetoric*,[2] which described the speaker, speech, and audience as the major elements in oral communication. Despite some modifications, notably the addition of the channel concept for conveying the message, Aristotle's description is still basic, if limited in detail.

A brief, well-known, and influential contemporary verbal model was posed by Harold D. Lasswell, who asked " *Who* says *what* in *which channel* to *whom*, with *what effect?*"[3] A descriptive model, the Lasswell question might have been enriched by the addition of the phrase ". . . to whom *with what purposes* and with what effect?" Such an amendment would provide a criterion by which effectiveness could be judged.

Other models combine words and diagrams in an attempt to specify relationships and proportions. One of the important contemporary models was developed in the Bell Telephone Laboratories by a mathematician, Claude Shannon, and a colleague of his, Warren Weaver, for application to electronic communication. Shannon described an information source which produces a message. The message is acted upon by a transmitter, which converts (encodes) it into a signal suitable for transmission through a channel or medium, such as air, a light beam, or a wire. The receiver converts (decodes) the signal back into a message and it is delivered to a destination.[4] An important emphasis of this model is its concern for encoding and decoding functions and

[2]Lane Cooper, trans., *The Rhetoric of Aristotle* (New York: Appleton-Century-Crofts, 1932).

[3]"The Structure and Function of Communication in Society," in *The Communication of Ideas*, ed. Lymen Bryson (Institute for Religious and Social Studies, 1948), p. 37.

[4]Claude Shannon and Warren Weaver, *The Mathematical Theory of Communication* (Urbana: University of Illinois Press, 1949).

for the channel. Since 1947 many other models have been pro-posed for particular purposes. One of the influential general approaches has been the Source-Message-Channel-Receiver model of David K. Berlo.[5] The Berlo model shows the influence of Shannon and Weaver and adds at least four important elements. Source and Receiver are described as possessing identical types of personal and social characteristics. The components of the message are presented in some detail. The words Source and Receiver are used to suggest a Stimulus-Response (S-R) relationship. Channel is discussed in terms of sensory experiences, such as seeing and hearing, rather than as mechanical means of conveying messages.

This book proposes a speech communication model that represents a further attempt to specify essential elements, particularly as they relate to a strategy of public speaking.

THE SPEAKER-SPEECH-CODE-RESPONDENT MODEL

SPEAKER	SPEECH	CODE	RESPONDENT
Cognitive Structure		Visual	Cognitive Structures
Attitudes	Content	$\updownarrow$	Attitudes
		Verbal	
Social Roles	Organization		Social Roles
Purposes		Interposed	Purposes
	Style	$\updownarrow$	
Sensory Experience			Sensory Experience
		Interpersonal	

[5]David K. Berlo, The Process of Communication (New York: Holt, Rinehart and Winston, Inc., 1960).

THE SPEAKER

If our goal were to describe a public speaker as a communication source, we might do it in many different ways. We could make a list of physical characteristics involving his age, sex, height, weight, and hair color. Or we might decide on demographic characteristics such as his place of residence, education, political affiliation, and religious preference. Viewpoints and systems for such a description are abundant; but the important criterion is "Which differences make a major difference in how the individual behaves as a communication source?" If we wish to learn this, we will probably need to know what the speaker knows, his pattern of likes and dislikes, and his relation to the groups of people in his environment. Out of these elements he is likely to evolve some communication purpose—some reason for saying what he has to say. And to this list we should add the complex phenomenon of sensory experience, such as seeing, hearing, and touching, because the source's knowledge of the outside world has come from his senses, however sophisticated or simple were the things he has seen, heard, and read.

We can probably talk meaningfully, then, about what the speaker knows and thinks, or more broadly, his *cognitive structure*; how he feels about things, or his *attitudes*; his relationship to other groups of people, or his *social roles*. We know that the speaker's *purpose* can be explained in terms of a need to change his environment in some way. Let us now examine these factors in some detail.

COGNITIVE STRUCTURE.

Since the earliest writing on the nature of man, there have been attempts to describe him in terms of conflicting or cooperating forces, such as the mind, body, and soul, or the passions and the will. This thinking had its effect on communication ideas. It led to a classification of purposes in terms of informing, persuading, convincing, and entertaining. The work of Charles Osgood and others[6] on the dimensions of meaning suggests that while both knowing and feeling are unquestionably present in all of us, they are so interrelated that it may be meaningful to study them as parts of a whole, rather than separate entities. Labels used by some psychologists to describe these two facets of human experience are *cognitive structure* and *affective, or attitude structure.*[7] Cognitive structure consists principally of those myriad bits and pieces of information and ideas that we have been accumulating since the beginning of our awareness: "Bright sunshine makes you squint. Columbus discovered America in 1492. Scrambled eggs are yellow. It costs five cents to mail a letter." But these cognitive elements are not randomly arranged in the central nervous system, like a heap of note cards which have fallen from a file.[8] This "supply" of information is in a constant state of change at the conscious level, as knowledge is discarded or forgotten and sensory experience brings us new data about the world. Furthermore, the *structure*, or relationship, of these cognitive elements is changing continually in what Theodore Newcomb has called "The Strain Toward Symmetry."[9] In the view of balance theorists such as Newcomb, Charles Osgood and Percy Tannenbaum,[10] Leon Festinger,[11] and others, one of man's primary concerns is to fit

[6]Charles Osgood, G. J. Suci, and Percy Tannenbaum, *The Measurement of Meaning* (Urbana: University of Illinois Press, 1957).

[7]In discussing the cognitive and affective domains of experience, we have relied heavily on Benjamin Bloom, ed., *Taxonomy of Educational Objectives, Handbook I: Cognitive Domain* (1956) and *Handbook II: Affective Domain* (1964) (New York: David McKay Inc.).

[8]*Bloom, Handbook I, Cognitive Domain*, pp. 30ff.

[9]"An Approach to the Study of Communicative Acts," *Psychological Review*, LX (November, 1953), 393–404.

[10]"The Principle of Congruity in the Prediction of Attitude Change, "*Psychological Review*, LXII (January, 1955), 42–55.

[11]Leon Festinger, *A Theory of Cognitive Dissonance* (Stanford: Stanford University Press, 1957).

the random and uncoordinated elements of his experience into patterns that are meaningfully consistent and predictable. This is not to suggest that an individual's cognitive structure is ever complete or finished. It cannot be for a least two reasons. One is the factor already mentioned—the continuous alteration of the supply of data. The other is that the individual's experience requires him to establish relationships between a very limited number of the total cognitive elements stored in his nervous system. He will probably never be required to relate "Abraham Lincoln" and "mashed potatoes," or palm tree" and "differential calculus." Other relationships, however, may have been repeatedly reinforced, such as "Republican Party" and "conservative politics," or "wet feet" and "common cold."

The cognitive structure of the speaker is thus the frame of reference out of which he must operate. He cannot choose from knowledge he does not have. He may possess only partial knowledge of an event and behave as though his information were complete. He may be so specialized in a particular matter that he cannot think about the situation of other people who do not share his understanding. In addition to the presence or absence of particular cognitive elements in his experience, he also will be affected by the relationships or analogies that he has been able to draw among the elements. Thus the ability to think in terms of analogies or similarities will be a part of the total cognitive equipment of the speaker. For a given speech, the speaker's knowledge of his own abilities and limitations, his perceptions of appropriate respondents, and his knowledge of how to construct and encode messages for particular audiences will be a part of his cognitive resources.

ATTITUDES.

A second important characteristic of the source, closely related to cognitive elements, is his attitudes. Attitude may be defined as "the predisposition of the individual to evaluate some symbol or object or aspect of his world in a favorable or unfavorable manner."[12] An individual not only knows things, but he has attitudes toward what he knows which strongly affect the value and importance he attaches to the knowledge. Many Americans familiar with rocket launchings know "attitude" in terms of the degrees a rocket leans in either direction from the vertical. We might borrow this concept to suggest that people "lean" toward or away from things they know about, or they are relatively neutral (vertical) concerning them. Attitudes seem to stem from these conditions: (1) The situation under which learning initially took place, (2) The degree to which later experience has reinforced or caused rejection of the information, and (3) Related attitudes and knowledge that are consistent with or different from a particular piece of information.[13]

An example may serve to illustrate the relationship of knowledge and attitudes. Suppose the knowledge is "ability to diagram a sentence." Suppose further that you first encountered this idea under highly unfavorable conditions—hot and humid weather, a stomach ache, and an irritable teacher. After one or two false starts, however, you were able to diagram a sentence satisfactorily. Furthermore, imagine that you again encountered it later in school under similarly uncomfortable conditions. You could still perform the diagramming function, but the unpleasant connotation stayed with you. In discussions with fellow students, you would be likely to sympathize with those persons who were highly critical of the assignment. You might observe that there seemed to be little relationship between ability to diagram sentences and high grades on essays and other written assignments. Thus your initial negative attitude about sentence diagramming had been reinforced by subsequent experience and by related events. Almost anything you now might say about the technique is likely to be negatively conditioned by your attitudes. In

[12]Daniel Katz, "The Functional Approach to the Study of Attitudes," *Public Opinion Quarterly*, XXIV, No. 2 (1960), 168.
[13]Bloom, *Handbook II: Affective Domain*, Chapter 3.

other situations, a highly positive attitude toward some knowledge may lead to unwarranted optimism about how others will receive the information.

The work of Osgood and his associates has contributed much to an understanding of how cognitive elements and attitudes are interrelated—how they interact in supplying meaning to the individual.[14] Osgood has theorized that every denotative or "pointing" meaning (in general, what we have described as cognitive elements) has certain connotative, or personal dimensions which are capable of being indexed. To measure a person's connotations for a particular concept (say, "abortion," or "Charles de Gaulle"), he is asked to express his reaction to the concept on several scales between pairs of polar opposites, such as: fair–unfair. After much experimentation, Osgood concluded that the most reliable dimensions of connotation could best be characterized as evaluation, activity, and potency. The best evaluative scale was "good–bad." Activity was measured best by "active–passive," and potency by "strong–weak." A measuring device consisting of several such scales is a "semantic differential." Semantic differentials have been used both to measure the locations of an individual's concepts in the "semantic space" and to make predictions about how messages sent to him are likely to be received.

A great deal of other research has been done in cognitive-affective relationships. In one experimental study involving college students, statements about Russia were provided and each student was asked to rate them on their truth or falsity and also on his approval or disapproval. The statements were again presented a week later, arranged this time into meaningful paragraphs. Then retention of the material was tested at several intervals over an eight-week period. When students believed a statement to be true and also had a favorable attitude toward the statement, or when they both disbelieved and disliked it, they tended to remember it. When a student believed but did

[14]Osgood, Suci, and Tannenbaum, *The Measurement of Meaning.*

not like the statement, or the opposite, he was less likely to remember it.[15]

In another attempt to examine the relationship of knowledge and attitude, subjects rated their own attitudes and knowledge of 30 nationality groups and then were given an objective test measuring their actual knowledge of the groups. When the subjects felt hostility toward groups, they tended to overestimate their knowledge; that is, they seem to have justified their dislike by believing that they knew more than they actually did.[16]

Attitudes exist, of course, not only toward factual matters which may be chosen for the message, but also toward the other elements in the communication process. The source's attitude toward himself, toward the act of composing and coding a message, and toward his listeners will all be a part of his behavior when he speaks. It is the fundamental unity of the organism on which this book bases its views about the effect of communication—to affect or change. As Martin Scheerer puts it, "Behavior may be conceptualized as being embedded in a cognitive-emotional-motivational matrix in which no true separation is possible."[17]

SOCIAL ROLES.

As a social being, a man finds himself joined to a great many groups, which are formal or informal, voluntary or involuntary, large or small. Some may be as general as a social class; others as immediate as a parent-child relationship. Each group exists for particular purposes and goes about fulfilling those purposes in certain ways. The group develops certain standards or tradi-

[15]Robert Garber, "Influence of Cognitive and Affective Factors in Learning and Retaining Attitudinal Materials," *Journal of Abnormal and Social Psychology*, LI (1955), 384–89.

[16]Joseph B. Cooper and Lawrence J. Michiels, "Study of Attitudes vs. Factors of Objective Knowledge," *Journal of Social Psychology*, XXXVI (1952), 59–71.

[17]*Handbook of Social Psychology*, (Cambridge: Addison-Wesley Press, 1954), p. 123.

tions, often labeled *norms*, plus specialized functions, or *roles*, through which work is performed. Both the norms of the group and the role that an individual holds will have a potent effect on his behavior as a speaker. For example, group membership will often determine what subjects a speaker may select, what position he may take on the subject, how he will compose and encode the message, and whom he will choose as respondents. Sometimes these choices will be consciously made with group norms and his roles in mind; often they will be made subconsciously, because group membership is so much a part of the speaker that he may not distinguish between himself-as-a-person and himself-as-a-group-member. Either way, group membership is a significant influence on choices.[18] In accounting for the communication behavior of a speaker, *what* he is in a group-membership sense represents as important a dimension as *who* he is in a cognitive-affective sense.

PURPOSES.

Within the broad framework of the desire to affect his environment, the speaker will have certain specific changes in mind. As in all good educational or communicative practice, the more specifically and functionally the speaker is able to identify his purposes to himself, the more likely he is to achieve his goal. Purpose is important for at least three reasons:

I. It represents a motivational device for the speaker. Presumably the attainment of his purpose will be rewarding to him. Thus a clear and manageable statement of objectives may help keep him at the task of preparing and presenting his message.

II. Purpose serves as one criterion for making decisions about

[18]For an extended discussion of social roles as a dimension of communication, see J. W. Riley and M. W. Riley, "Mass Communication and the Social System," in Merton, Broom, and Cottrell, *Sociology Today* (New York: Basic Books, Inc., 1959), pp. 537–78.

what will go into the speech. If we are able to verbalize our purpose in terms of one or a number of specific acts that respondents are to perform before we can regard the communication as successful, then we have a useful set of criteria, though certainly not a recipe, for procedure. If we accept this idea, then a speech purpose such as "I want to increase the students' concern about cheating on this campus" is not adequate. The expressed purpose might be particularized into: (1) Students should know about surveys of cheating on this campus; (2) Students should know about statements on cheating made by campus leaders, faculty, and administration; (3) Students should know about cheating on other campuses; (4) Students should develop a definition of what constitutes cheating; (5) Students should hear a summary of the disadvantages of cheating; or (6) The next time a student is tempted to cheat, he should remember the speech and evaluate the possible consequences of cheating. All of these specific purposes are possible and reasonable. They can serve as a guide to the collection of material and the composition of the speech.

III. Purpose is a standard against which a speaker can assess the feedback or result of his initial efforts and help him decide what additional speeches, if any, need to be made to accomplish his objectives. Feedback may also have the effect of causing the speaker to modify his initial purposes.[19]

SENSORY EXPERIENCE.

The factor of sensory experience is included as a reminder that the speaker learns about the world through the medium of the senses, which can be fallible and selective. An observer can never know everything about the situation he wishes to describe. His ability to see, hear, touch directly is limited to one vantage

[19]For a further discussion of purpose and feedback, see Winfred Hill, *Learning: A Survey of Psychological Interpretations* (San Francisco: Chandler Publishing Company, 1963), pp. 199–202.

point at a time. The data he obtains may be further reduced in completeness and accuracy by inattention or lack of sensory acuity. His ability to analyze what his respondents are doing is subject to the same limitation. Sensory experience is a vital link between the source and his environment.

THE SPEECH

Training in public speaking and writing has always placed a heavy emphasis on the *message* as the key to communication success. This continuing concern has led to the development of many rules for message-making. They include ideas about form such as correct grammar and syntax. Concepts of organization include the use of an introduction, a statement of purpose or proposition, an internal system of organization, and a conclusion. One of the most pervasive ideas about message content has been that communication purpose is a central aspect of the message itself. That is, there are speeches to inform, persuade, convince, and the like, and this matter is determined primarily by what the message contains, rather than how it is received. Many of these message ideas are useful because they give the speaker or writer guidelines on how to proceed. They are undesirable only if they fail to contribute to the purposes that both source and respondent bring to the communication situation.

In the view presented by this book, the development of a speech derives from three matters. One is purpose: both the purposes of the speaker and the purposes that he assigns to the respondent. The second is the data which the speech describes. The other we might label "social reality testing." This is the realization that sooner or later the speaker's statements will be compared with the observation of a situation which others have made. Reality testing is important because the speaker with a high commitment and enthusiasm for his purpose may have his perceptions distorted to a degree that will render his message unacceptable or unintelligible to persons who do not share his views. Or the speaker may have such sensitivity to the respondent's purposes that he will describe the situation in misleading terms. An effective counterbalance to the speaker's attitudes and purposes is the perception of others about the realities of the matter under consideration. In a political environment of free speech and press, and of high mobility for both messages and people, actual or anticipated "reality-testing" by auditors is a potent influence on most public-speaking situations. It is the force most likely to keep the speaker "honest" in his accounts.

A useful and traditional view of speech development is to describe the speech in terms of content, organization, and style. Quantitative studies in content analysis, readability indices, and the order of presentation in persuasion have tended to bear out the validity of these divisions. Content may consist of verbal descriptions of events, numerical or statistical data on events, or opinions by people who are identified as authorities. These units must appear in some relationship or order. The source will choose how the units are to be organized. In addition to choices about units of information and how they are arranged, another set of choices will involve the words to be employed and their placement in sentences of various types and length. Just as content choice will be a product of purpose and of reality-testing, decisions concerning organization and style will be indicated by characteristics of the respondents.

THE CODE

Unlike a report or a book, a speech must be spoken aloud, in public, in order to come into being. This fact introduces another set of decisions, which we have labeled *code*. Part of any speech will be visual because the speaker is both seen and heard. Beyond this necessary connection of the visual and verbal, the speaker will choose to code his message further in some combination of oral and visual presentation. That is, he may decide merely to speak all the words he uses, or he may reinforce or clarify his spoken words by means of pictures, written words, graphs, or the like. A common fallacy is the assumption that *every* speech can be made more effective through visual reinforcement of the content. The fact is that effectiveness may be materially reduced by use of visual stimuli in certain cases. A speech that is (or must appear to be) spontaneous can be compromised by the use of visuals. Moreover, because of their communication styles, some groups or audiences may regard visuals as inappropriate or undesirable. One code choice, then, is a balance between visual and verbal presentation.

A second set of code alternatives involves the "closeness" between speaker and respondents. We will label as *interpersonal* any relationship in which the speaker and listeners are all physically present and can hear and see one another without amplification or other mechanical aids. Although there is admittedly some difference between a situation involving one speaker and one listener and another involving one speaker plus fifty listeners, in either instance both parties may continuously adjust to the response of the other and questions may be asked and answered. When we introduce mechanical amplification, we begin to interpose barriers between free interaction of source and receiver. When speaker and audience are physically apart and are connected by television or radio, a truly *interposed* system may be said to exist. Immediate feedback now becomes impossible.

When interposed codes are used, the directness and intimacy of interpersonal conditions are sacrificed to gain a much larger number of potential respondents. But the enlarged audience is bought at a price. On the encoding side, the speaker is no longer able to use subtle cues from the audience that guide his pace and timing, suggest places where content or wording changes might be required, or indicate momentary effectiveness. On the decoding side, the listener is no longer able to exert momentary influence over the speaker's behavior, because the amount and kind of cues passing between speaker and listeners and between groups of listeners themselves are reduced. Thus, to achieve a given impact in the interposed situation, the speaker must plan more carefully and anticipate audience reaction in greater detail.

One exciting notion which is relevant to choices about code is Marshall McLuhan's idea that communication media can be categorized as "hot" to "cold." A medium that leaves little to be filled in or completed by the listener is "hot." "Hot" media include radio and newspapers. "Cool" media, such as telephones and speeches, require greater activity by the audience to complete the message. This is true partially because of the number of cues each medium provides, but more importantly for another reason. Radio and print media tend to have a stereotyped formula and style for presenting information. Take a story about an auto accident or an international crisis. The aspects of the event to be reported have been determined by almost endless repetition. The language is stereotyped as well, so that the only variability occurs in such matters as names, dates, and places, and the manner in which these data are to be presented is also predetermined. Because the message is almost totally predictable or redundant, the respondent has to do almost nothing. "Cool" media lack this high degree of redundancy and predictability and so require the respondent to be more active.

We have all experienced speeches that were so "cool" (required us to supply so much completion in terms of our level of comprehension) that we gave up after a few minutes, in confusion and frustration. We may also have suffered in the presence of a speaker whose ideas and words were so predictable and redundant that no participation was required by us. Perhaps we were offended because the speaker had underestimated our capacity to understand. The speech was too "hot." Between these extremes is a realm of choice about the "hotness" and "coolness" needed for a particular audience. Both the code alternatives presented here, verbal-visual and interpersonal-interposed, are functions of the "temperature" of a message.[20]

THE RESPONDENTS

The word "respondent" has been used to describe the other persons in a speech situation, in order to emphasize that a person hearing a speech plays an active, rather than a passive role. He does not merely receive; he reacts. The terms that describe characteristics of the speaker are also applicable to the respondents. This is not to suggest that the two are alike; only that they can be discussed in the same way.

COGNITIVE STRUCTURE AND ATTITUDES.

Before discussing respondent characteristics and how they are likely to affect the message, we may do well to note David Kretch and Richard Crutchfield's comments on the interaction of attitudes and cognition: "There are no impartial facts. Data do not have a logic of their own that results in the same perceptions and cognition for all people. Data are perceived and interpreted in terms of the individual perceiver's own needs, own emotions, own personality, own previously formed cognitive patterns."[21]

The interaction of attitudes and cognitive elements in the respondent is likely to produce the following effects:

1. The respondent will interpret the speech in the context of his past experience. He will compare the events described with other events in his memory and will apply the same or similar cognitive characteristics to the message whether or not such a fit is appropriate.

2. The respondent will interpret the speech in a way that will not threaten strongly held attitudes or cognitive elements.

[20]Marshall McLuhan, Understanding Media: The Extensions of Man (New York: McGraw-Hill Book Company, 1964).

[21]Theory and Problems of Social Psychology (New York: McGraw-Hill Book Company, 1948).

Enthusiastic members of political parties deal with propaganda from the opposition by ignoring it. If they hear a message with views favorable to both sides, they tend to remember items supporting their views and forget the others.

3. If a message lacks completeness or if some of the details do not seem to form a comprehensive pattern, the respondent will complete and regroup them in terms of his experience. That is, he will systematically alter the message to make it fit his cognitive structure and attitudes.

This interaction is, of course, not entirely complete. An individual cannot have attitudes toward cognitive elements he does not possess. Speeches cannot evoke or change meanings not already present. So cognitive elements and attitudes will function separately to some degree in determining how a respondent may be affected by a speech. The point is that achievement of the speaker's purpose will depend on (1) what the respondent knows and (2) how he feels about it.

SOCIAL ROLES.

Just as what the speaker says is determined in part by the groups he belongs to and the roles he occupies in those groups, so the responses available to the respondent will be fixed to a large extent by his group memberships and the parts he plays within them. Far from being free agents, we are also perhaps family members, Republicans, Methodists, members of lodges or fraternities, students at a particular university, and many other things. Each of these groups in which we are actively involved brings us in contact with specialized ways of looking at the world, uses some of our energy, and makes our responses somewhat more predictable.

PURPOSES.

The person who finds himself in the role of audience member will possess purposes relative to the speech being given. These purposes may be similar to, in opposition to, or totally irrelevant to those held by the speaker. They also may be less or more well-formed and rigidly defined. Respondent purposes may often be thought of in terms of expectations. A church member might attend a service expecting the sermon to cast new light on his personal problems. A student who nears the end of the term with low grades may go to the summary lecture in a course hoping to make up some of his deficiencies. A concerned citizen might attend a lecture on American foreign policy expecting to hear potent new ideas for dealing with Communism. A student may go to hear an extremist lecture out of curiosity, or in order to be able to boast later about his open-mindedness. Of course, the speaker may have other purposes from those held by the audience members. If in the process of working toward his own goal he also meets the needs of respondents, then no conflict results and a high degree of satisfaction is achieved. But if speaker and respondent want different and incompatible things, or if both have the same purpose and the speaker does not succeed in fulfilling it, then purpose becomes a problem.

In summary, respondents as well as speakers bring purposes to the speech occasion. Whether the speaker succeeds in producing the change he wants in the respondent may depend on whether their purposes coincide or conflict.

SENSORY EXPERIENCE.

Even though the speaker may give important ideas which he needs to talk about and has given particular attention to the style, content, treatment, and code of his speech, he has access to the respondent only through sensory experience—what the audience can see, hear, and perhaps touch. For this reason, the amount of redundancy—the repetition or predictability of the message in the words used and in visual reinforcement of verbal stimuli—may play an important part in success.

There is evidence in the work of Adelbert Ames,[22] Jerome

22"Reconsideration of the Origin and Nature of Perception," in *Vision and Action*, ed. Stanley Ratner (New Brunswick, N. J., Rutgers University Press, 1953).

Bruner and Leo Postman,[23] and others that the senses are not an "open window." They are modifiers of the outside world, and may either add to or reduce what is "really" there. Things are seen and heard in terms of past experience with seeing and hearing similar things. Thus there may be a difference between what a speaker says and what people hear him say. This may be a barrier or an aid to achievement of purpose.

SUMMARY

The respondent and speaker are affected by the same interpersonal and intrapersonal variables. Speech reception is subject to the cognitive elements and attitudes present in the respondent, as well as the respondent's group memberships and social roles.

Assignment: Setting Up a Plan for Communication

On your college campus or in your home community, you probably perceive some matters that seem to require a program of planned change. Figure out a communication strategy for the program, using the six steps contained in Chapter II.

1. Which are the primary and secondary audiences to whom speeches should be addressed? What priority should exist?
2. Using available information about the attitudes, knowledge, beliefs, and actions of each potential audience, is it possible to reach some tentative conclusions about the amount of acceptance or rejection that is likely?
3. What is the nature of your knowledge, attitudes, and beliefs on the subject?
4. In general, what is the nature of the messages that must be formulated for the program?

[23]"Perception, Cognition, and Behavior," in *Perception and Personality: A Symposium*, eds. J. S. Bruner and David Kretch (Durham: Duke University Press, 1955).

5. How should the speeches be delivered? What are the verbal, visual, and mass media possibilities for presenting the speeches?

6. How can evaluation and follow-up be used in helping to determine how well the objectives have been met?

Be prepared to present this strategy by means of a paper or oral report.

chapter 3

THE SPEAKER

AND THE

WORLD

AROUND HIM

Chapter 2, with its discussion of strategy and communication models, suggests that much of the speaker's task is analytical. There are two things which we *do not* mean to imply by this approach: The first is that the formulation of strategy and the application of a model is exclusively an armchair operation. Although it may involve some quiet contemplation and note-making, it will also consist of active observation, interviewing, and review of pertinent materials. The second is that this phase is something to be completed and set aside in favor of other, more practical matters. The observation that "there is nothing so practical as a good theory" applies here. Further, the selected strategy needs to be subject continuously to revision as new data become available. The description of the situation contained in the model will become incomplete or inaccurate with the passage of time, even during the speech itself. So if there is a task that extends through the entire speech-making process, it is planning and evaluation.

This chapter implicates the same continuity, for it involves the changing relationship of the speaker and the world around him. The focus is different, however, because here we will be concerned with that portion of the speaker's observations he may consider appropriate for introduction into his speeches.

Having discussed such abstract matters as communication strategy and models, we might assume that it would now be possible to move to a specific, nontheoretical activity—the collection of information for the speech. If the speech is a classroom exercise and the speaker is casually selecting a topic from among a range of alternatives in which he is not an expert, he is indeed likely to go through a specific period of information-gathering. He will make a choice and then look for data in his own experience and in the library. If the speech situation is a real one, however, the process of information-gathering will not be bounded so definitely in time and space. The speaker's attitudes, cognitive structure, group memberships, and commitments as a change agent will all have been operating. He will not choose or be asked to speak about matters foreign to his concern. Thus preparation for a particular speech has been going on during the whole period of the speaker's awareness of a matter. For the speaker in a real situation, information-gathering is not merely a chronological step that falls between the choice of subject and the speech delivery. It is an integral part of him. He may make his knowledge more specific or update it through research. But preparation will be a continuous, ongoing process both before and after the speech is delivered. Why after the speech? Because in an ongoing program of communication for change, each speech becomes a part of the background of subsequent speeches.

THE NATURE OF INFORMATION

An important dimension in information-collecting involves the nature of data itself. A traditional "objective" viewpoint concerning information is that physical reality is more or less directly available to the observer. If he is sufficiently skilled in observation and his vocabulary is adequate to the task, his account of an event may be treated like the event itself. In this view, the only variable to the truth of a statement is the competence of the reporter. By contrast, there are "subjective" philosophies, which deny even the existence of the individual, generally on the grounds that we cannot conclusively prove that we exist, nor that the world around us has any existence other than that which we give it. Such a position treats reality as a manifestation of mental activity. Both the objective and subjective positions have definite limitations for the public speaker. The objective view ignores the inaccessibility and complexity of the physical world, the inadequacy of language when we try to describe direct experience, and the preconceptions which the observer brings to the event. And the subjective view raises some practical problems. The person whose thigh bone has been severed by the impact of an automobile has no choice but to behave as though he has a broken leg. A subjective view about his nonexistence will not serve him very well.

Regardless of his viewpoint, the investigator will form a set of propositions about the world, which he tends to treat *as if they were* the real world. Yet the statement he formulates in his mind is not the event that he saw or heard. Further, the observation on which the statement is based is subject to certain limitations.

The first limitation is human physiology. Man cannot see "light" of certain wave lengths, nor can he hear more than a limited range of sounds. He may use mechanical devices to extend his ability to examine reality, but instruments, too, have their limits. Even under ideal conditions, including the presence of trained observers and favorable conditions of observation, we can never see and hear all that is available. Our nervous system is so constructed that we can only take in a certain amount of information at one time. Thus, whether the subject of a speaker's commitment is a particular political candidate, a product to be sold, or a subject to be taught, the store of information available to the speaker will be necessarily incomplete.

A second limitation on man's ability to observe the world is his psychological nature. Here we do not refer to ways in which the organism is constructed, but to internal determinants of perception resulting from past experiences. Beliefs, attitudes, and idea structures help determine what items we will select from our perceptual field, and which we will ignore. Psychological factors of perception operate as a complex screening device, allowing some stimuli to come through and others to go unnoticed. As George A. Kelly, a psychiatrist, expresses the idea, "Man looks at his world through transparent patterns or templates which he creates and then attempts to fit over the realities of which the world is composed."[1]

Within these general conditions of psychological structuring, we have hypothesized a further specific condition on the observer—a strong commitment to introduce change. Thus the speaker's viewpoint may cause him to inject or eliminate observations and statements concerning matters in which he is deeply involved.

A third limitation on the information available about any event or experience occurs when the observer attempts to report his observations. Statements about an event can only approximate the observations that have been made. The statements will be both incomplete and distorted by the nature of language he must use. Thus any speaker who sets out to learn more about a situation or event by personal observation or through the reports of others should first be careful to disengage himself from the idea that he will learn the "truth" or successfully report it to others.

Because scientists are aware of the imperfections of human observation, they impose upon their investigation conditions of rigor that public speakers may find uncomfortable and unnecessary. One basic tool is the concept of probability. Since certainty is not available, scientists refer to what degree they feel confident that a particular outcome might be typical of the total population of such events. This confidence is often expressed in terms of probability. For example, a number of studies appear to show that under certain conditions women are slightly more persuasible than men; but how great must be the difference observed in a particular study before we are willing to say that the results are due to some difference between the sexes and not to chance or random variations in our measurement of persuasi-

[1] The Psychology of Personal Constructs (New York: W. W. Norton & Company, Inc., 1955), Chapter 1, pp. 8f.

bility? Powerful statistical tests are available which will tell us the *probability* that the difference in a given experiment was due to chance alone. If the experiment has been carefully set up, then this probability figure can help us to reach a decision about differences in persuasibility between the sexes; for if the calculated chance probability is extremely small (say, 1%), then we are led to believe that some underlying difference between the sexes—not chance accidents of sampling of measurement—is responsible for the observed difference. Implicit in these statistical procedures, however, is the requirement that the conclusion be accepted only tentatively; after all, the test tells us in the foregoing example that there exists a finite possibility—a probability of 1%—that our results are in fact due entirely to chance. The 99% probability that the results are *not* due to chance gives us considerable confidence in the hypothesis of some real difference between the responses of the two sexes in our experiment; our confidence would have been greater if the probability had been 99.9%—that is, if the chance probability had been 1%. Such a degree of precision in expressing probability is seldom possible in the matters with which the speaker must deal. He may, however, profit from adopting the probability viewpoint by asking, "What seems to be the probability that the set of statements I have assembled is adequate to describe the events about which I must talk?" Because probability is the outcome of attempts to describe anything, therefore, thorough investigation is of utmost importance to the speaker.

THE NEED FOR INVESTIGATION FOLLOWING COMMITMENT

Through direct experience and through awareness of the experience of others, the change agent has come to his commitment and acceptance of responsibility. In other words, he evidently already knows enough about the situation to have caused cognition and attitude formation in himself. There are at least three reasons why he needs to know more:

I. What produced change in him may not be sufficient to cause a similar change in his respondents. It may be difficult, moreover, for him to achieve their frame of mind. He cannot reconstruct his experience back to the point at which no attitude formation had taken place in him. He cannot consciously recall how he felt before he played his first game of golf or made his initial decision to vote Democratic. Therefore, he may have difficulty in estimating the kind and quantity of statements necessary to stimulate attitude change in others regarding such matters. Furthermore, what he can consciously recall may not be the evidence that produced the change in him. The sensitive change agent will be aware of the perils of assuming that because he possesses a strong attitude it will be easy to bring others to the same attitude.

II. He may need to know more in order to evaluate his own attitudes and knowledge. Perhaps the experience that influenced the forming of his attitudes was not typical of the total experience available, or perhaps the situation has changed considerably since his original contact with it. This would complicate the task of changing others who have had dissimilar experiences. Such evaluation by the change agent may cause him to alter the nature of his commitment. He may become more aware of the difficulty that his proposed change represents for others. On the other hand, if further investigation seems to support his position, he will probably be more confident and effective as a public speaker.

III. Most important, perhaps, the speaker must have available the broadest possible choice of evidence from which to construct his messages for maximum effectiveness. There are at least three reasons for this:

1. He must be prepared to overcome resistance to change in the respondents. If resistance is present, the speaker must ask himself why his listeners feel as they do. The speaker must

possess information that will enable him to identify his views with the experiences of others.

2. In many speaking situations the speaker will encounter stated or implied opposition. Perhaps his opponent is a recently published newspaper article or a broadcast which most of the respondents have encountered. Or it may be the threat of a new tax levy hinted at by the legislature. Or it may be a hostile questioner. Whether physically or psychologically present, the opposition must be confronted with a more effective statement of views. This refutation may often be dependent on superior knowledge, either of the charge or of the position being attacked.

3. Every committed speaker operates with the necessity of presenting the most defensible propositions about his subject and avoiding those that have limited supporting evidence. (The same does not apply, of course, to the uncommitted speaker, who presents his tentative views in the hope that audience responses will help him to explore his knowledge and beliefs more thoroughly. But our concern here is with the committed speaker.)

There is some experimental evidence to indicate that when a source uses unsupported assertions, his receivers see his trustworthiness as lower than when the message includes supporting materials.[2] The prudent professor will not often present a lecture in which the key points are contrary to the belief system of his discipline. Nor is the dedicated politician likely to admit that his tax program may lead to bankruptcy for the state. If he has done an adequate job of data collection, he will know where his position is vulnerable and where he can emphasize his views with confidence.

[2]J. W. Brehm and D. Lipsher, "Communication-Communicatee Discrepancy and Perceived Communication Trustworthiness," *Journal of Personality*, XXVII (1959), 352–61.

THE PRIORITY FOR INVESTIGATION

If the speaker decides he needs more information, a common assumption is that he will lay aside all other roles and devote his time and energy to investigation. Perhaps unfortunately, this choice is almost never available, despite a high feeling of responsibility. He has other roles to perform. The college student, for example, chooses among speech preparation, assigned reading, other subjects, employment, and social responsibilities. The amount of time he allots depends less on the total time available than on the position of speech preparation in his value system.

Even with a high level of speaker motivation, however, the time period between commitment to speak and the date of the speech may limit the amount of specific preparation. All the material that would contribute to an understanding of the subject may not be capable of assembly in the available time. And some time must be allotted to decisions about what data to use and what to hold in reserve, and how the chosen material can be organized effectively. Some time must be allowed for practice of the speech. In the presence of these demands, therefore, what is the best way to proceed with further collection of information?

At a point early in the preparation process, the potential speaker will find it necessary to take an inventory of what he knows about the subject, his attitudes toward that knowledge, and its relation to the anticipated audience. This inventory will help him decide whether he needs to look beyond his personal resources for information. It may also reveal that more up-to-date material is required, that his own favorable attitudes may have resulted in the stretching of limited data beyond what would otherwise be acceptable to a listener, or that there are possible new directions for investigation.

Let us emphasize that at no time will the investigator be engaging in an objective cross-sectioning of available data such as a scientist might attempt in obtaining a random sample of persons or events. If he is sincere in his commitment, the investigator will place higher value on discovering material that supports his position, and lower emphasis on contrary data, though contrary information may be highly useful for answering arguments or anticipating opposition. At least the distortion will be in a direction favorable to his commitment and this will be to his advantage in presenting his views.

The Role of Direct Experience

Personal data—that is, the experiences and attitudes of the speaker which have been developed through his personal relationship with the subject under discussion—should be given high priority as evidence. This is particularly true if the source occupies a role perceived by his receivers as being highly related to the subject under discussion.[3]

A form of direct experience, but one which possesses some different characteristics from the speaker's observation, consists of personal interviews with persons who are already known or who can be identified as credible sources of information. The personal interview presents the data collector with the opportunity to probe more deeply for data on potentially useful points and to seek from his sources new approaches and insights. Interview materials will also enhance the credibility of the speaker because they suggest that he is close to the center of activity and has access to contacts which may be both private and pertinent. The interview, of course, is not without its limitations. The speaker may have difficulty in establishing contact, especially with a person of high responsibility. The greater the person's importance, too, the more difficult it may be to obtain specific statements, especially on controversial matters and questions of policy. Interviews are often expensive in time and energy, and they cut into available time for speech preparation. We may also

[3]Jean S. Kerrick, "The Effect of Relevant and Non-Relevant Sources on Attitude Change," Journal of Social Psychology, XLVII (1958), 15–20.

assume that the committed investigator will find some meanings in the statements of the interviewee that support his own views but are not necessarily intended. When the possibilities for observation and interviews have been reduced, written accounts by other sources should be considered.

Assessing the Statements of Others

In deciding how far investigation should carry him beyond the bounds of his knowledge and interview information, the data collector should raise the question of how adequate a model of the event his present knowledge represents. In other words, does he have enough information yet to assure himself that his verbal description corresponds generally with events in the world as others are likely to see them? Do the data already gathered meet the goal of "reality testing"?

Having answered this question, one can proceed to a more detailed assessment of other data. One of the first distinctions which we may be able to make is the difference between accuracy and credibility. *Accuracy* results from an adequate system of observation and description, rigorously applied. *Credibility* is our tendency to accept a report of something because we trust and believe in the person or group who made the report. As speakers we can be grateful that an audience believes in our credibility or in the acceptability of our sources of information. As data collectors we should resist the attraction of credibility until we have investigated as well as possible the methods by which the information was obtained.

A major concern of the data collector should be to assess the nature and extent of error present in the data he has received. Most people probably have negative connotations for the word "error," relating it to "bad," "wrong," or "to be corrected." The term is not used here as a value judgment. Instead we mean to equate "error" with "not a complete and accurate description of an event." The discipline of logic supplies us with two categories for classifying statements. These categories are *true* and *false*. Most of us would say that "The world is flat" belongs in the *false* category, whereas "The world is round" should be described as *true*. Of course, it is not true that the world is round (a geometrically perfect sphere). But the second statement is so much less in error that it will serve the communication purposes of most speakers and respondents. A geophysicist could generate a set of words and figures for his colleagues that would represent a highly detailed description of the earth's surface. But his description would only approach accuracy (defined as the actual shape of the earth). The data collector needs serious answers to the somewhat facetious question, "How wrong can you afford to be?" Because an object or event being talked about is different from the statements used to describe it, let us consider some of the ways in which a statement can be in error. It may be:

1. *Incomplete*—some aspects of the event will not be included in the report.

2. *Distorted*—because of the nature of language and the ways in which it must be utilized in making statements, some aspects of the matter being described will be emphasized more than others.

3. *Out of date*—The account will not reflect a current version of the events which have occurred. No physical or social process stops. It keeps releasing energy and generating effects or it transmutes itself into other forms. Verbal accounts, being static, cannot reflect this process. They only "photograph" something that was there at a particular time and place.

4. *Inaccurate*—The account may contain descriptions of phenomena which were not observed by anyone, but which were projected into the description because of the past experience of the observer.

This may sound like an unnecessarily pessimistic view of man's attempts to describe his environment. Yet it is an essential perspective for the data collector if he is to be armed against the self-delusion that he has captured the truth in his observations and that those who disagree with him have failed to do so. When he speaks, he will treat many of the statements he makes as though they were free from error; at the preparation stage he should be operating from a more guarded point of view.

If the errors in any statement or group of statements help to support a certain conclusion, for example that something should be encouraged or prevented, then a type of error called *biased* has been operating. If some aspects support a conclusion and others appear to deny it, then the error is probably *random* in nature. Again, no value judgment is implied. By *biased* we mean only "pointed toward a particular conclusion," and by *random* we mean "not oriented in any particular direction."

This way of talking about the nature of error has been applied so far to statements of factual description. Its use becomes more obvious when we apply it to statements about what will or should happen in the future. Error is a necessary part of prediction or advocacy, because we consciously close off other possible courses of action and specify the one in which we believe or which our commitment requires. If we are interested in learning about the prospects and limitations of a system of government-sponsored medical care for the American people, for example, the official statements of the American Medical Association will doubtless attract our attention and may possess high credibility for us as we are information-gatherers, as well as for the potential respondents to the speech we give. Yet if we confuse credibility with freedom from bias, we are in some difficulty. The American Medical Association has made a commitment to its members and to the public to oppose government intervention in medical care. If we are to analyze the statements of AMA officials on this topic, we will be left in little doubt that the Association's position is one of biased error on this issue. Proponents of government health care plans have likewise consciously chosen to engage in biased error in describing such plans and the AMA's reactions to them.

Although most groups in our society operate from the position which we have labeled as biased, there are some organizations which are committed to a scrupulous nonpartisan position. They attempt to assemble information and analysis for the citizen without advocacy, expressed or implied. The Brookings Institution is such an organization. We would expect to find its analysis of a situation in error, but in the form that we have labeled random. Its accounts will differ from the actual events, but the statements will not differ in a fixed and predictable direction. Such sources may not be of maximum assistance to us in our role of advocate, but they are highly useful when we are operating at the investigative level, because they help us to assimilate opposing viewpoints on an issue and to examine more closely events in the physical world.

The credibility of information sources whom respondents perceive as "objective" or "fairminded" is also worth examining as a clue to investigative, as well as speaker, behavior. Repeated claims of objectivity appear to increase the credibilty of the source. Furthermore, if a speaker presents some material that differs from his announced position, this act appears to increase the probability that he will be believed.[4]

THE "AGE" OF A PUBLIC ISSUE

In the course of events, people are born, they exist, and they die. During their existence they affect and are affected by their environment. If they impress persons around them in a favorable way, we often label them "important"; or if they become prominent and antisocial, "notorious" may be our description. They may become known in every country around the world, or they may never be heard from outside their home community. Some live to extreme old age; others perish in infancy. So it is with ideas. Some are global in their concern and appear in the history of every age. Others remain almost the exclusive concern

---

[4]T. N. Ewing, "A Study of Certain Factors Involved in Changes of Opinion," *Journal of Social Psychology*, XVI (1942), 63–88.

of their authors and perish when their sponsors die. The amount of exposure that an idea has had is a matter worth noting in the information-gathering process.

There appears to be a close correlation between the number of times a matter has been publicly discussed and the number of persons who remember having heard it before. According to one research program on public knowledge of political issues, people spent more time discussing "older" topics. Later interviews disclosed that a number of issues newly introduced through the mass media at the time of the earlier interviews had now become topics of conversation and had taken on the characteristics of "older" arguments. There were fewer contradictory viewpoints regarding "new" arguments which had just been introduced by press and radio than regarding "old" issues which had been more thoroughly discussed and thought about.[5]

We believe that it may be helpful to the investigator, therefore, to give some consideration throughout his preparation to the "age" and "social standing" of his subject.

If a speaker is a specialist, in, say, scuba diving or income tax reform, he may have a tendency to project his values onto the potential respondent and to assume that the subject is both older and more important than it may be generally perceived. In fact, we believe that age is one of several related concepts. These concepts include kind of information, amount of information, and language available. They may be placed on continua as follows:

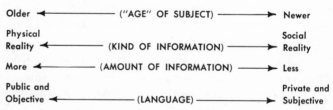

[5]Douglas Waples and Bernard Berleson, "Public Communication and Public Opinion," in G. Leigh, *The Conceptual Framework of Public Communication* (Mimeo), 1954.

What we are suggesting is that older ideas, that is, those which have been matters of investigation and public awareness for a relatively long period of time, will have generated more information about the physical events surrounding the matter, that relatively more information of all kinds will be available, and that language available for discussion of the subject will be more objective and public. Newer subjects will tend to generate information of a social reality type, partly because the number of observers will be more limited and also because they are likely to have made an early commitment; less total information will be available, and the language for discussing the ideas will be less formalized and more personal, with fewer generally accepted public meanings for the words employed.

The public is presently becoming aware of the existence of sky-diving clubs. These organizations are composed of persons who follow a prescribed set of rules and procedures for jumping from airplanes. Information about the clubs is limited mostly to personal accounts by participants and occasional mass media coverage devoted to pictures of jumpers. Since the activity is relatively new, little research or analysis of records has been conducted by outside observers, and most of the information available comes from the social reality experienced by the jumpers, who use a specialized vocabulary, which is largely connotative and personal, to describe their activity. A member or nonmember who makes a commitment to speak about these clubs from any viewpoint will tend to encounter a relatively small amount of data, mostly socially oriented, produced by heavily committed spokesmen, and expressed in a connotative, specialized vocabulary. Much of the data on parachute jumping would be subject to what we have termed *biased error.*

For purposes of contrast, let us speculate on what experience a change agent who has a commitment to speak on trends in theories of raising children might encounter. He would discover a time span extending from the beginnings of human history and he could take counsel from Buddha, Plato, the authors of Proverbs, and Dr. Benjamin Spock. The volume of information would be beyond his capacity to assimilate directly, but he would find compilations, tabulations, and comparative treatments which would tend to modify social reality as perceived by the sources and to be more related to the physical reality. He would also discover a large body of social science research devoted to observation of child-rearing. While he might encounter wide differences in approach to the study, he would also become aware that the language used to describe events tended to be somewhat standardized and public. His over-all impression of the data would be that it should be viewed as *random error*, since almost every conceivable contradictory and counteractive position would be represented.

SUMMARY

The preparation of a speaker for a particular speech has been going on since he first became aware of the situation that he would discuss. Direct observation is conditioned by physiological and psychological variables in the observer. The speaker's commitment will also strongly affect what he sees and fails to see. He will need to take a careful inventory of his own knowledge and attitudes in deciding whether further investigation is necessary. The amount of additional research will necessarily be limited by the other roles the speaker possesses.

If the assumption is made that all observations are in error because they are in various ways incomplete or inadequate to represent the event, then the investigator will distinguish between data that reflect *biased error*, or are partisan, and information that involves *random* error, or lack of evident partisanship. Another important determiner of data is the "age" of the matter under consideration. The amount and kind of information, as well as the language available to discuss it, are functions of the age of the topic.

Assignment: Discovering the Nature and Extent of Error

Chapter 3 presents a view of information about any event as being either random or biased in error. If this view is meaningful, then it should be possible to determine to some extent the nature of the error in a given account.

1. Select a front-page newspaper story for a test of this idea. To what extent is it incomplete, distorted, out-of-date, or untruthful? What can you conclude about the factor of error? Does it appear to be esentially random or biased in nature?

2. Prepare a speech or oral report which includes the story, the evaluation of evidence, and a defense of your conclusion about the factor of error.

chapter 4

THE

MACROSTRUCTURE

OF SPOKEN

MESSAGES

This chapter contains some of the most specific and prescriptive material to be found in the book. Message structure has been dealt with in this way because the authors believe that it lends itself to such treatment more readily and realistically than does almost any other variable in the speech communication process. Message structure is necessarily a linear one-thing-at-a-time matter, although as statements accumulate they take on a multidimensional aspect, as we will see in Figure 15.

The task of structuring a speech consists of converting into a message the collection of statements that originally grew out of investigation. Factors affecting the problem of which statements are to be selected for a particular communication purpose will be discussed mostly in Chapters 5 and 6. An approach to how the statements may be structured, also in part a content decision, is to be found in Chapter 4. The experience of gathering and formulating statements for potential use in the speech is likely to have generated in the speaker's mind an appealing order or sense of direction. This order may be based on the actuality of which events were discovered first, which second, etc. Or it may be related to the volume of data about different aspects of the matter to be discussed. This order may by chance turn out to be the ideal arrangement for a particular speech. But we cannot be very sure of this until the topic has been analyzed in some systematic overall manner.

Internal structure is characteristic of messages of all types— musical compositions, paintings, computer programs, sculptures, and architectural designs, as well as such verbal messages as poems, novels, plays, lectures, and political speeches. When we say that a message has internal structure, we are asserting, first, that upon close examination it may be decomposed (or analyzed) into identifiable parts, and second, that these parts are arranged in some pattern of relationship to one another.

Speeches in particular are highly structured. Much of their patterning occurs at what is usually called the "linguistic" level, where the units are such language elements as phonemes, morphemes, words, phrases, and sentences, and where the relations are linguistic ones such as the rules of syntax. Because these elements are relatively small segments of the whole, we may refer to the linguistic structure of a speech as its "microstructure."

But patterning may be seen on a larger scale at what has usually been called the "rhetorical" level. The units of rhetorical structure include such elements as statements of main points and subpoints, transitions, introductions, examples, and the like. Because these elements are relatively gross segments of the whole, we may refer to the rhetorical structure of a discourse as its "macrostructure." In this chapter, we shall examine certain features of macrostructure in spoken messages, with a view to understanding its nature and function.

STRUCTURE AND CONTEXT

Before taking up the structure of verbal messages, we will do well to look more closely into what is meant by "structure" and how it contributes to certain effects that are of interest to the speaker.

Perhaps the most significant feature of structure is that it creates a situation in which each element of the message is set in meaningful context with the other elements of the message. Before we see how this applies to speeches, let us see how certain general principles of context operate in a trivial, but instructive, graphic example.

Figure 1 is a graphic message containing eight elements. Some

FIGURE 1

of them are quite familiar to you, and none of them is particularly hard to grasp, yet if you were to close the book and try to reproduce all eight, you would find it hard to do so. (You would find it even harder if the preceding two sentences had not emphasized that there were eight elements in the figure.)

One reason why Figure 1 is so hard to remember is that it is rather weakly structured. This is not to say that it is entirely unstructured, for it is divided into eight discrete elements (remembering that there are eight of them makes the task of reproducing Figure 1 easier), and some of the elements are familiar figures. But they do not create any context for one another.

What might be done to provide more structure for this figure? Let us begin by considering one element in what might be called "zero context":

FIGURE 2

G

Standing in isolation, this element appears to us as one of 26 items in our alphabet. Examined closely, it is an arrangement of curved and straight lines; but ordinarily we see it as a single thing, the capital "G." Within the context of the letter, the individual lines lose their identity and blend into a single familiar configuration. The letter forms a context for the lines that make it up, but in Figure 2 the letter itself does not appear in any context.

However, let us add a capital "O" following the original "G": Without altering the letter itself in any way, we nevertheless

FIGURE 3

G O

have changed it in some important ways. "G" in "go" is not the same as "G" in isolation; the difference is not in the letter, but in its context. It is perceived as a *part* rather than a *whole*. Now, it represents one of two sounds making up the English word, "go."

But suppose we add another "O" to the two letters we already have:

FIGURE 4

G O O

Except to the trained phonetician, who hears a difference between the "G" sound in "go" and the "G" sound in "goo," we have not changed the "G" significantly; but we have changed the "O" substantially. Instead of representing a speech sound in its own right, it now combines with the second "O" to represent a completely different sound: its status is changed from that of a *part* (the representation of the "oh" sound in "go") to that of a *subpart* (one part of the representation of the "oo" sound in "goo").

We may carry the same process a step further by adding a capital "D" to the first three letters:

FIGURE 5

G O O D

Now the original "O" is part of a different sound altogether, for the "oo" sound is changed from the low front vowel of "goo" to the middle vowel of "good."

Up to this point, each succeeding addition has made a significant new pattern, within the context of which the significance of the old pattern, itself physically unaltered, was changed. Not every addition would produce an equally meaningful result. For instance, we could now add the letter "K" to the four we already have:

FIGURE 6

G O O D K

By adding the "K" most readers would say we had produced nonsense; they would find the string of letters "GOODK" meaningless, slightly irritating, and difficult to remember. We would have gotten a different result by adding below the four letters the straight line from Figure 1:

FIGURE 7

G O O D
—

Unlike the "K," this addition is not particularly irritating. But it is equally meaningless and hard to remember. If one is not looking carefully, it is likely to be overlooked, and it is likely to be regarded as superfluous. However, by adding the remaining elements from Figure 1 in the right configuration, we may endow this line with significance and transform the entire graphic representation into a radically different kind of message:

FIGURE 8

The meaningless line is now a mouth. What were formerly the letters "G" and "D" now appear as ears, and the "O's" are now eyes.

Several important points should be noted concerning the effects of context observed in these figures. First of all, though we ordinarily expect complex things to be more difficult to grasp than simple ones, you probably noted that Figures 2, 3, 4, 5, and 8 are about equally easy to recognize and remember, even though each is more complex than those preceding it. This seeming violation of our expectations is explained by the principle that wherever possible *we tend to see familiar patterns as unitary wholes rather than as collections of parts.* Indeed, evidence from perceptual experiments shows clearly that even if some of the elements are left out of a well-known pattern we still tend to perceive the pattern itself rather than the remaining constituent parts. Since the capital letter "G," the word "GOOD," and the cartoon face all are recognized as familiar patterns, each may be handled as a single unit of perception, memory, and thought, even though the cartoon face contains more information and represents a more complex arrangement of elements than the other figures. Thus, *a familiar whole is recognized and recalled almost as easily as any of its parts.*

No doubt you also noted that Figure 8 is considerably easier to recognize and recall than Figures 6 and 7, and very much easier than Figure 1, even though it contains more elements than Figures 6 and 7 and exactly the same elements as Figure 1. The differences here are attributable to the same principle: despite its complexity, Figure 8 may be conceptualized as a single entity, but in Figure 7 there are two separate entities to notice (the word and the line), and in Figure 1 there are eight. Individuals will differ with respect to the ease with which they recognize and recall Figure 6, depending upon whether they see it as two elements ("good"+"K") or five ("G"+"O"+"O"+ "D"+"K"). This suggests that *difficulty of recognition and recall depend more upon the number of recognizable whole patterns than upon the number of individual elements making up the task.* Thus, a relatively large number of elements may be perceived and recalled more easily than a smaller set of the same elements, if the larger set is composed into a single coherent pattern and the smaller set is not.

Figures 1 through 8 also demonstrate that *the meaning, sig-*

*nificance, or character of an element is determined by its rela-
tion to the whole context in which it is embedded.* The context
affects not only how we perceive the element, but also how we
remember it. If asked to reproduce Figure 8 from memory at a
later time, many of us would show the two circles as horizontally
flattened ovals [⬭ ⬭], because we would remember them as
"eyes;" but if asked to reproduce Figure 5, most of us would
draw the circles as vertically flattened ovals [◖◗ ◖◗], because
we would remember them as "O's."

As we saw in Figures 1 through 5, *an existing pattern may be
changed into a new one by adding meaningful elements*; but in
comparing Figure 5 with Figures 6 and 7, we also observed that
*nonmeaningful additions to familiar patterns either destroy the
integrity of the pattern or else are perceived as superfluous.*

DECOMPOSITION OF A VERBAL MESSAGE

Having observed some of the principles of context at work in
simplified form in a graphic example, we may now turn to their
operation in a verbal message. We begin by examining a short
talk addressed to a group of students enrolled in a required
course in public speaking. Whereas in the former instance we
composed a structured figure from elements, in the following
example we will reverse the process and decompose a structured
speech into elements. Our method will be to divide the whole
speech into its largest constituents (that is, into the smallest
number of parts into which it can be separated), then to divide
each of the parts into its constituents, and so forth until the
analysis has been carried as far as it seems profitable to go.

Following this procedure (and ignoring for the moment the
underlined material in the figure), the first stage of analysis sep-
arates the speech as a whole into three primary divisions, numbered 1, 2, and 3. The largest of these parts, 2, develops the
major substance of the speech. That is, Divisions 1 and 3 seem
to add nothing to the major points the speaker apparently is

FIGURE 9
DECOMPOSITION OF SAMPLE SPEECH

(1) I'm sure that a good many of you would just as soon not be here this morning. Some of you would prefer to be spending this time getting some of your math requirements out of the way. No doubt there are others who figure that the time could be used more profitably in some of the many extracurricular activities which the university provides for the cultivation of our physical, mental, and social well-being. Or maybe you'd just rather be at home in bed. In any event, some of you may be wondering this morning just why your college, department, or special curriculum requires you to be here, enrolled in a beginning course in public speaking.

(2) Now, the ways of the faculty are strange indeed, and I doubt that even the dean of your college could give you all the reasons why you're here this morning; certainly I can't. But I can give you three reasons. They are the three that keep cropping up whenever deans, department heads, and curriculum directors come to us with the news that a speech course is going to be required in a new program of studies. There may be other reasons, but the three I want to tell you about this morning have become so common that we've come to expect them as a matter of course.

DIVISION 1

64

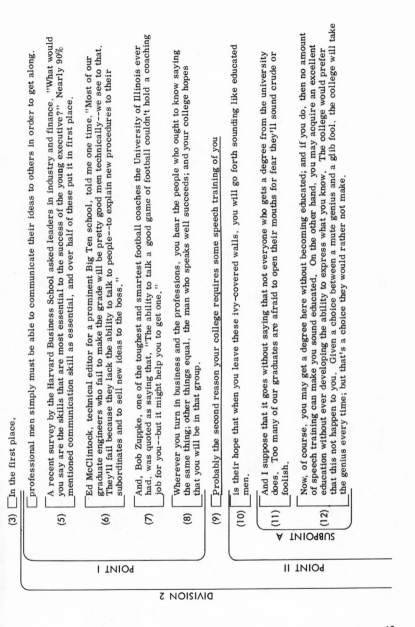

(3) In the first place,

(4) professional men simply must be able to communicate their ideas to others in order to get along.

(5) A recent survey by the Harvard Business School asked leaders in industry and finance, "What would you say are the skills that are most essential to the success of the young executive?" Nearly 90% mentioned communication skill as essential, and over half of these put it in first place.

(6) Ed McClintock, technical editor for a prominent Big Ten school, told me one time, "Most of our graduate engineers who fail to make the grade will be pretty good men technically--we see to that. They'll fail because they lack the ability to talk to people--to explain new procedures to their subordinates and to sell new ideas to the boss."

(7) And, Bob Zuppke, one of the toughest and smartest football coaches the University of Illinois ever had, was quoted as saying that, "The ability to talk a good game of football couldn't hold a coaching job for you--but it might help you to get one."

(8) Wherever you turn in business and the professions, you hear the people who ought to know saying the same thing; other things equal, the man who speaks well succeeds; and your college hopes that you will be in that group.

(9) Probably the second reason your college requires some speech training of you

(10) is their hope that when you leave these ivy-covered walls, you will go forth sounding like educated men.

(11) And I suppose that it goes without saying that not everyone who gets a degree from the university does. Too many of our graduates are afraid to open their mouths for fear they'll sound crude or foolish.

(12) Now, of course, you may get a degree here without becoming educated; and if you do, then no amount of speech training can make you sound educated. On the other hand, you may acquire an excellent education without ever developing the ability to express what you know. The college would prefer that this not happen to you. Given a choice between a mute genius and a glib fool, the college will take the genius every time; but that's a choice they would rather not make.

POINT I

POINT II

SUBPOINT A

DIVISION 2

65

POINT II

SUBPOINT B

(13) A good part of your speech training is devoted to just this job--helping you to sound like an educated man.

(14) When your speech instructor tells you, "Stand straight and put your weight on both feet when you talk," what he's really saying is, "Stand the way a mature, educated person would stand if he were to make this speech."

(15) When he tells you to pronounce words clearly, he's telling you to conform to one of the most provocative status--cues of the educated middle class in the United States.

(16) When he insists that you set your speech apart in separate main points, he is not only helping you to communicate your ideas more effectively, but he is also requiring you to form your ideas in the way that educated men have used since the time of the ancient Egyptians.

(17) Not only do your advisors hope that your course in speech will help you to learn to communicate more effectively and to approach more closely the speech standards of the mature, educated person, but they also want you to have some practice, early in your college career, in formulating your ideas into words and presenting them orally to your fellow students.

POINT III

SUBPOINT A

(18) Most college students, especially at the freshman and sophomore level, fail to realize how much talking they'll have to do in order to get through college. But consider the following points:

(19) In virtually every course you take, you will be graded in part on the quality of your class participation, which takes place through the spoken word.

(20) In about a fourth to a third of your courses, you will be required to present at least one short oral report to the class.

(21) In one or two of your advanced courses in the major, you will probably be called upon to present a long report, or to be responsible for a whole class period.

SUBPOINT B

(22) Obviously the speech-trained students perform better in these tasks than the students who have never been before an audience of other students.

(23) I remember a student whom I taught several years ago at Florida State University when he was an undergraduate and I was a graduate student working on a Ph.D. He wasn't the best speaker I ever had, but he worked hard. Last spring I met him here on the Wisconsin campus. We went for coffee, and he told me he had started to work on a Master's in education. He told me that, on the average, he was making a major oral report once every two weeks, and he also told me that it was pretty easy to pick out those in his classes who had received some speech training before entering graduate school.

(24) What this student told me merely confirmed what a good many administrators on every campus believe: that a speech course in the freshman year often improves performance in later college work.

DIVISION 2

(25) Now, I have tried to acquaint you with the three reasons most commonly given for the required speech course in the pre-professional curriculum: First, because professional men must be able to communicate in order to succeed, and your college hopes that you will succeed; second, because your college hopes that you will leave it sounding like an educated man, and the speech course can help you to do that; and finally, because much of your advanced work in college will be through the medium of the spoken word, and a little training in speech now may pay big dividends in improved performance in advanced courses in your specialty.

(26) Let me say that I wouldn't want to rest my whole case for speech training on these three advantages of the beginning course. I might even say that I personally see some reasons for teaching the course which are stronger in the long run than any of these. But these are the reasons college administrators most often given for requiring their students to take the course. In all probability they are the major reasons why most of you are here this morning. And they are the reasons why, if any of you ever become deans, department heads, or curriculum directors, you will be very likely to require that all of your freshmen take a basic course in public speaking.

DIVISION 3

trying to make; they could be discarded and the speech would lose no essential information.

This does not imply, however, that Divisions 1 and 3 are useless; they are what we usually call the "introduction" and "conclusion." They add substantially to the effect of the speech in two ways. First, they serve to place the whole content of the speech in context with the listener's motives and present frame of mind, so that the speech is not a disembodied, abstract essay but is connected with experiences and ideas *outside* the speech (this is especially true of Division 1). Second, they emphasize what the main points of the speech are, provide a central idea around which these points revolve, and show how the main points are related to it (this is especially true of Division 3). We will return to these two functions later. First, Division 2 requires further analysis.

Division 2 is what would ordinarily be called the "body" or "development" of the speech. It divides itself readily into three segments, labeled I, II, and III, each of which holds the content related to one of the three main points. Using a similar principle of division, Points II and III may be subdivided further into two smaller segments each, called A and B in each case. Following conventional terminology, we would call these smaller segments the subpoints of the speech.

To summarize the first three stages of analysis, we have now divided the entire composition into three major *divisions* corresponding to introduction, body, and conclusion. We have thus far concentrated attention on the body, which has been divided into three *main points,* and two of these have in turn been divided into two *subpoints* each.

Now we are in a position to divide these segments into still smaller ones. Let us examine the content of Point I in closer detail. The segment may be decomposed into five elements: a statement (4) that professional men need to be able to communicate; a quotation (5) of statistics from a survey supporting statement 4; a quotation (6) from a faculty member supporting statement 4; a quotation (7) from a football coach supporting statement 4; and an assertion (8) that restates 4 in more elaborate terms. Since all of the content of this segment of the discourse seems to be associated with segment 4, it might be regarded as the "statement of Point I"; segments 5, 6, and 7 might be regarded as "supporting materials for Point I," and segment 8 might be called the "restatement of Point I."

Further decomposition of these elements might be possible, but it would require linguistic methods, which would move us from analysis of the macrostructure of the message to analysis of its microstructure. Our macroscopic analysis reveals, then, that Point I consists of a statement of point, followed by three example-quotations used as supporting material, followed by a restatement of point. When similar analysis is made of each of the subpoints within Points II and III, the structure of each subpoint is found to differ somewhat from the others; II-A, for example, consists of no more than a statement of point followed by one contrast developed as supporting material.

When the analysis is completed, it is possible to display the result in a variety of ways. Figure 9 is no doubt one of the more cumbersome; a more convenient way of depicting it is the "outline" in Figure 10.

THE REPRESENTATION
OF CONTENT ELEMENTS AND RELATIONS

After years of formal schooling, most of us grow so accustomed to using the format of Figure 10 that we come to regard outlines as the only natural way of summarizing the content of a discourse and expressing "logical" relations among ideas. However, the outline was completely unknown to the earliest writers on both logic and speechmaking. It is in fact a fairly recent innovation. And, though it is one of the most useful inventions since the wheel, its use—far from being natural or inevitable—is a learned art.

FIGURE 10
OUTLINE OF THE FIGURE 9 SPEECH

SUBJECT SENTENCE: College administrators see three main
advantages of taking a speech course
early in one's college career. (2) (26)

I. Professional men must be able to communicate well. (4)

      Example: business survey (5)
      Example: engineering instructor (6)
      Example: football coach (7)

II. An educated man should sound like an educated man. (10)

    A. Not all educated persons sound educated. (11)

        Contrast: mute genius vs. glib fool (12)

    B. Speech training helps one to sound educated. (13)

        Example: posture norms (14)
        Example: pronunciation standards (15)
        Example: organization principles (16)

III. A speech course in the freshman year improves performance
in later college work. (24)

    A. Most students use speech regularly in their courses. (18)

        Example: classroom participation (19)
        Example: short oral reports (20)
        Example: long reports in advanced courses (21)

    B. Speech training improves oral classroom work. (22)

        Example: graduate student's experience (23)

The essence of the outline is *abstraction*: a short phrase or
sentence characterizes a much longer segment of the discourse.
Thus, Statement I is an eight-word sentence in Figure 10 that is
used to characterize a 210-word segment in Figure 9. Each identifiable segment of content in the speech is represented in abstract or abbreviated form by a sentence or phrase in the outline.
(Exceptions to this rule are introductions, transitions, restate-
ments and conclusions, which will be discussed separately.)

In the discourse, some segments are subdivisions of longer
segments. The inclusion of one part within another is shown in
the outline by indentation: the *levels of subdivision* in the speech
are represented by the *levels of subordination* in the outline. In
Figure 10, the three "examples" are indented under II-B be-

cause they represent immediate subdivisions of segment II-B in the speech; II-A and II-B are indented under II because they summarize units that are included within that segment. Thus, the outline not only shows the division of the discourse into parts, but also displays the arrangement of parts within the whole and of subparts within the parts.

The outline is by no means the only way of showing these relations. For instance, the subdivisions could be shown equally well by a topological graph such as in Figure 11. Indeed, Figure 11 enjoys one advantage, in that the nesting of subparts within parts and parts within the whole is somewhat more obvious there than in the outline. However, Figure 11 suffers from two serious drawbacks. First, it is more difficult to construct and to interpret; it is unlikely that so laborious a procedure would have come into very widespread use as a means of describing message content. More important, however, is the fact that the outline is capable of conveying more information about the speech because it contains a dimension of structure that is missing from the topological representation:—sequential arrangement. This is important because the sequential arrangement of parts is a vital feature of all spoken messages.

Thus far, we have regarded the outline as a means of representing the *content segments* of the speech. Because this representation is done in abstract form, it would seem logical to say that the outline represents the *main ideas* of the speech. But the very features that make it so useful for representing segmental units render the outline an imperfect way of representing ideas; for subdivision and sequence, which are indispensible features of speech segments, are not at all characteristic of ideas.

First of all, it is profoundly misleading to think of ideas as if they were divided and subdivided in categorical relationships to one another, like the parts of a discourse. It is more profitable to regard each idea as an individual thing that is connected with other ideas in a variety of different ways. Whether Idea A is subordinate to Idea B is not an absolute question, but is dictated by

FIGURE 11
TOPOLOGICAL REPRESENTATION OF FIGURE 9 SPEECH

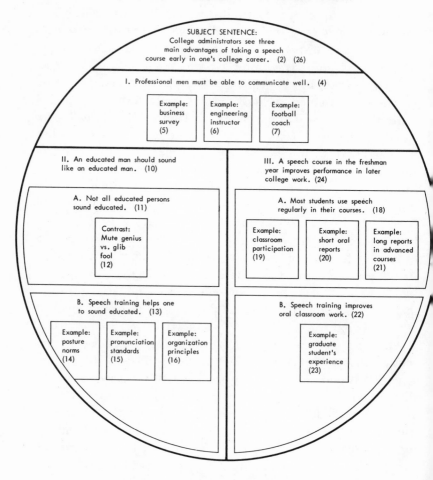

the context in which the question is asked. This concept, at first glance, appears to defy common sense. Most of us, for instance, would defend the notion that "whale" is a subdivision of "mammal"—not in any relative sense, but absolutely. And so it is in the following context:

What are the types of mammals?
  Horses
  Cats
  Whales
  etc.

We say that "whale" is a subdivision of "mammal" because this is the context that usually comes to mind when the question is posed. But consider the following context:

What are the characteristics of whales?
  They are the largest living animals.
  They live in the sea.
  They are mammals.
  etc.

In this context, "mammal" is subordinate to "whale"; it is one of many ideas brought to mind by the idea "whale." Neither *idea* is in any wise a "constituent" of the other, except in the sense that the two ideas are connected to one another through a conventional zoological classification system.

The same principle is confirmed by the speech outline in Figure 10. It includes the sequence:

S.S.: College administrators see three main advantages of taking a speech course early in one's college career.
  II. An educated man should sound like an educated man.
    B. Speech training helps one to sound educated.

This suggests that the idea "Speech training helps one to sound educated" is subordinate to the idea "An educated man should sound educated"; and within the context of this speech, the subordinate relation does hold. But consider the following arrangement:

S.S.: It is desirable for the college student to take a speech course.
  I. It helps the student sound like an educated man.
    A. Some jobs are open only to persons who sound educated.

B. Many doors open socially to the person who
sounds educated.

C. It is fitting that a college graduate should sound
educated.

II. It confers increased powers of self-expression.

Within this framework, the subordinate-superordinate relation
between these two ideas is exactly reversed.

Another reason the outline is an imperfect way of representing ideas is that it is misleading to think of ideas as if they were
arranged in sequential order. The outline may correspond to the
discourse in this respect, but certainly not to the ideas as such;
the relations among ideas are simultaneous, not sequential. As
a representation of the *ideas* of the speech, Figure 12 is superior
to an outline.

Because it concentrates on *relations* among ideas rather than
order of presentation, Figure 12 is more representative of the
ideas of the speech as they were held by the speaker prior to the
speech and, hopefully, as they will be held by the listener afterward. Moreover, it clearly shows that the speaker has not only
the job of presenting the ideas, but also the task of presenting
the relationships among them. Not only does Figure 12 show
us that the major content of the speech consists of 19 ideas
arranged in an unambiguous pattern around a single "central
idea" (the Subject Sentence), but it also shows us some important features of the interrelations among ideas. For instance,
it is clear that the ideas expressed by elements 11 and 13 are
related to one another in the context of this speech by virtue
of their mutual relations to element 10, and that their relation
to the Subject Sentence is not direct, but occurs because they
are connected to 10, which in turn is connected to the Subject
Sentence. It is this whole interrelated pattern of ideas that the
speech is designed to establish in the minds of the listener.

It is, then, possible to represent the content of a speech in
either of two ways, depending on whether it is viewed as a seg-
mented document or a set of ideas. The outline of Figure 10,

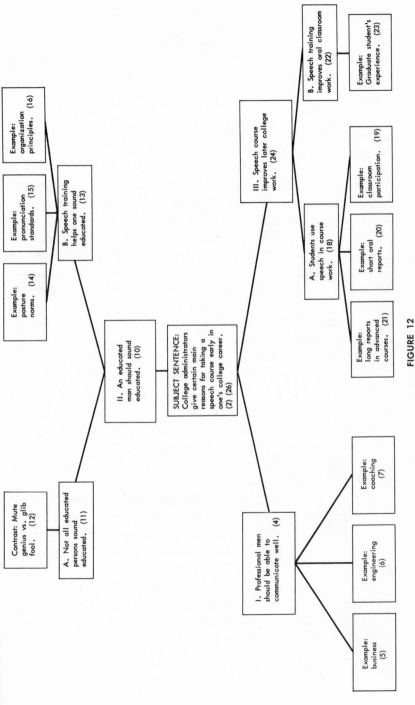

FIGURE 12

CONNECTIONS AMONG THE IDEAS OF THE FIGURE 9 SPEECH

reflecting subdivision and sequence, is an effective way of representing the speech as a document. The diagram of Figure 12, reflecting simultaneous interrelation, is an effective way of representing the speech as a constellation of ideas.

Content as Idea Structure: Analysis and Synthesis

Speakers usually talk about topics to which they have devoted considerable study and systematic thought. We may view a person's image of such a topic as an interrelated pattern of ideas and associations, and his object in speaking as presenting that pattern, or some part of it, to an audience. Only rarely will he be able to retrieve the pattern or a satisfactory portion of it in an acceptable order on the spur of the moment. In order to guarantee that he has pulled out those elements and relations that will be most useful to him and most meaningful to an audience on a given occasion, the speaker performs an operation usually called "analysis."

The term "lysis" means breaking apart, or breaking down into fragments. "Analysis" refers to a process of deliberately breaking something apart for the purpose of studying its components and their relationships. Sometimes analysis is performed by separating components physically, as in "qualitative analysis" in chemistry, in which a compound is systematically decomposed, literally broken apart. Sometimes, however, analysis is performed without actually taking the object of analysis apart, as for instance in "market analysis" in commerce and industry. In the first case, one manipulates the elements themselves; in the second case, he manipulates symbols that represent the elements.

The elements of a speaker's image of a topic are ideas. Now, in recent years it has been fashionable to question whether there exists in fact any such thing as an idea, and if so, just what it might be. We may avoid philosophic and psychological disputes by saying that for present purposes an idea may be defined as that within the speaker which makes it possible for him to generate a coherent unit of discourse. According to this definition, there is an idea behind (or in, or implied by) a coherent sentence, paragraph, or utterance. The idea is not equivalent to the utterance, for the same idea may be expressed in different ways; the idea is an abstraction from the utterance. While this definition does not solve any psychological or philosophical problems, it does permit us to use the term "idea" in a way that is useful in understanding the content and construction of speeches.

When we speak of "analyzing a topic" as a stage of preparation for communication, we refer to a process of isolating ideas that are part of the speaker's image of the topic, representing them symbolically, and examining the relations among the symbols. At least, that is what we mean when the speaker has a well-formed image of the topic; when he does not, "analysis" means something a little different, as we shall see below.

ANALYSIS.

What makes analysis possible is the fact that ideas for the most part exist not in isolation, but in context with one another. For a given individual, some connections between ideas or concepts will be essentially nonlogical: due to accidents of conditioning, stimulation of one idea leads to occurrence of another. However, of greater interest here are associations that might be termed "logical." By "logical" we do not mean necessarily "valid" or "correct," but simply the existence of some recognized relation between two concepts. Such relations form the kind of connecting links for idea structures that are regarded as suitable for incorporation in messages.

Consider, for instance, the concept, "juvenile delinquency." For any given individual, that concept is linked to others in a variety of ways. Two of these ways are "cause" and "effect"; anyone who has read or talked much about the topic has several ideas about causes of juvenile delinquency and about its effects. To many people, for example, "poverty" is one concept that is linked to juvenile delinquency as a cause, and "economic waste" is linked to it as an effect.

Other ideas are in turn linked to these. Connected to the idea of poverty as a cause of juvenile delinquency may be a remembered quotation from a prominent juvenile judge that poverty fosters juvenile crime (authoritative support), figures showing that an unusually high proportion of juvenile offenders come from impoverished homes (statistical support), and a statement of a juvenile offender stating that he felt he had nothing to lose by breaking the law (anecdotal support). Connected to the idea of economic waste as an effect of juvenile delinquency may be the contrast between the parasitic existence of the institutionalized delinquent versus the economic contribution of the average young citizen, and statistics showing the added cost of police protection due to juvenile crime.

The idea cluster described in these terms is represented graphically in Figure 13, in which the circles represent what might be called "substantive ideas" and the lines represent various kinds of relationships connecting one substantive idea to another. It is these relations that provide coherence and internal context to the idea cluster. Given such relations, the set of ideas has some logical structure; without them, it is a random assortment.

Consider, for example, the addition of an idea, "Boys' Town is a home for delinquent boys." It is clear that there is no convenient place for that bit of information in the idea structure outlined above; the "Boys' Town" idea standing alone is out of context with the other ideas: that is, it bears no immediate relation to them. If it were to be made a part of the idea cluster, then some relation would have to be found between it and some other idea in the pattern. One might form such a relation by considering "solutions" to the problem of juvenile delinquency: one solution is resident homes for delinquents, and Boys' Town

FIGURE 13
PARTIAL IDEA STRUCTURE
FOR "JUVENILE DELINQUENCY"

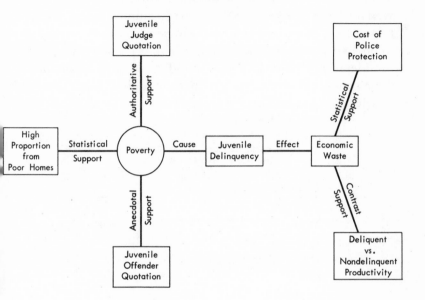

is an example of the resident home concept. Awareness of these relations might motivate one to consider other solutions, or other examples of this particular solution.

From the above considerations it would appear that a useful way to analyze an idea structure is to consider abstract relations such as cause, effect, example, contrast, problem, solution, definition, and the like. According to one's audience and purpose, some set of relations might be chosen to serve as a basis for questions leading to a logically related cluster of ideas. For instance, as noted above, one could use the substantive concept of delinquency and the abstract relation of cause to generate or call to mind other substantive concepts. The essence of this procedure might be represented by Figure 14, showing how the question,

"What causes juvenile delinquency?" creates an incomplete pattern into the context of which one or more completing elements might be placed. To put the question is to assume that one has available some concept "X" that will complete the pattern of Figure 14. The pattern could be reiterated as many times as one could find different X's to complete it. Then on the basis of considerations about the audience and the purpose of the speech, those connected ideas most pertinent to a given occasion could be selected.

FIGURE 14
**STIMULATION OF CONCEPT
THROUGH ABSTRACT RELATION**

SYNTHESIS.

It is obvious that the technique we have shown here to be useful in analyzing an existing idea structure may be equally useful for growing a new one. One might never have thought about the causes of juvenile delinquency before; but by asking the question represented in Figure 14, he may be stimulated to add to his thinking about the question. Although addition of new elements to one's idea structure in this way proceeds in a fashion that is similar to the analysis of existing images, it is clear that something more is involved. The speaker in this latter instance is called upon to supply information and connections that he has never had available before. This kind of "analysis" does not proceed by breaking apart an idea structure, but by building one up. It might better be called "synthesis."

RESEARCH.

If the speaker seeks his missing elements in books, newspapers, interviews, or other data collected according to procedures outlined in the last chapter, then his activity may be characterized as research. He may do this research either before or after he begins the task of synthesizing an idea structure, or he may carry on the two operations together. If the speaker is very sure about the relations he wants to rely upon, he will ordinarily pose questions such as the one represented by Figure 14 before he begins research operations, and he will direct his efforts only to finding the missing specific bits of information. He may find, for example, that he needs only two or three good examples of juvenile delinquency to complete an otherwise satisfactory idea structure, and in this case he will conduct his research so as to locate the missing examples as efficiently as possible, paying very little attention to other information that he may encounter on the way.

Once relationships are formed and an idea structure begins to grow, the speaker will be more alert to those ideas and bits of information that fit conveniently into the existing idea structure than to any which do not. If he begins to build the idea structure prematurely, that is, before enough data are at hand, he may produce a distorted or superficial treatment of his topic.

So, if the speaker is not at all sure about what relations and ideas are available to him on a given topic, he may begin by collecting a great deal of information before trying to develop any systematic idea structure. Only after considerable data are in hand will he begin looking for relationships.

Usually research and synthesis proceed hand in hand. Research provides data; data suggest new relations; new relations suggest a need for further data, and so on. Moreover, these processes are frequently enhanced by creative thinking. Whenever the speaker undertakes to supply a missing element or connection by the formulation of new ideas, then he is engaged in creative thinking. Because it is so seldom possible to synthesize a completely coherent idea structure out of readily available concepts and relations, growing an idea structure almost invariably involves a measure of creativity.

GENERAL VS. SPECIAL RELATIONS.

It has sometimes been thought that it should be possible to devise a relatively short, manageable list of abstract relations such as cause-effect, problem-solution, etc. which could then be applied to any topic so as to generate a rationally interconnected cluster of ideas about it. Ideas could then be selected from the cluster for incorporation in a message designed to achieve a given purpose with a particular audience on a certain occasion. One reason why efforts to produce such a list of general relations have so far failed is that in almost every field of thought there has grown up alongside these general abstract relations a set of special relations peculiar to that subject matter, which allow for a much more penetrating analysis. For example, the "Stimulus-Response" relation is generally more directly relevant to analyzing psychological questions than other kinds of questions. In questions of policy, "advantage-disadvantage" relations are especially important.

Although one may analyze a topic in a special field through use of such general relations as those mentioned in this section, the resulting analysis is very likely to be superficial. Becoming educated in a new field of thought involves not just learning the substantive concepts of the field, but also learning the special kinds of relations that may be obtained in it. The informed speaker does a better job of analyzing a topic, not just because he has more information at his disposal, but also because he has more appropriate relations available and so can ask more penetrating questions.

Analysis of the topic is done in order to guarantee the availability of a well-organized and appropriate set of ideas to be incorporated in a speech. The process of composition then consists of developing a segment of discourse to correspond to each element in the idea structure, arranging these in some order, and adding rhetorical elements to show their relationships.

Content as Discourse: Arrangement and Composition

THE TEMPORAL SEQUENCE PROBLEM.

We may imagine that the ideas the speaker wishes to communicate to his audience are arranged in his thinking in some simultaneous relation to one another, but when he speaks he is restricted to producing messages that consist of a temporal string of segments. It is possible to show simultaneous arrangements rather easily with pictures, graphs, and diagrams; but because language must be produced one sound (or in the case of writing, one letter) at a time, it is much more difficult to show such arrangements with words.

We may wonder why it is important that the listener understand the structural relations in a speech. In most cases, shouldn't it be enough for him to get the individual elements and to structure them however he sees fit? In rare cases this may be both possible and sufficient. Ordinarily, however, unless the listener senses the place and function of the elements within the context of the whole speech, he will not comprehend fully what is being said at a given moment; and even if such understanding of individual elements were possible, he would not recall the content of the speech so well as if he also understood the structural relations.

In a sense, the structural connections between a given message element and the others to which it is related are part of its own meaning or significance. This is inherent in the principles of context. Whether a circle is an "O" or an "eye" depends upon the context in which it appears; the meaning of the circle is incomplete unless its context is understood. In much the same sense, in the sample speech (Figure 9) the meaning of segment 11 is explained in part by segment 12, and even by segments 13, 14, 15, and 16. Moreover, its significance is controlled in part by the fact that it is one of two ideas relating directly to segment 10. Thus, exactly what it means to say in this speech, "Not all educated persons sound educated," is derived not just from the statement itself, but also in part from its relations to other statements within the whole context of the speech. If that context is not understood, the statement will be misinterpreted.

In addition to the problem of interpretation, the listener also has the problem of recall. The problem of storing and subsequently retrieving the information contained in a long verbal message is an impressive one. Only rarely will the listener store the ideas in an arrangement that corresponds to their temporal order of presentation in the speech; on the contrary, ideas will be stored according to their "logical" connections. If the speech structure is not clear, then these logical connections among ideas will be missing, and individual items of content will be lost or dissociated from the rest of the speech.

In short, a grasp of the structure of ideas in a message is important because it contributes both to the immediate comprehension and understanding of individual speech elements, and to the recall of speech content. To the extent that it interferes with correct transmission of the idea structure of the speech, the temporal sequence problem is a significant one. When the idea structure is stringlike and consists of no more than a few elements, the sequence problem will be trivial. For this reason simple chronologies (such as narratives, descriptions of processes, and instructions for performing simple sequential tasks) represent, from a structural point of view, the least complicated sort of message. It is usually easy to construct message segments corresponding to the events, stages, or operations involved; and since the temporal sequence of the speech will follow exactly

the temporal sequence of the thing being described, the ordering of segments requires no special planning.

But where the relations among ideas are more complexly
ordered (as in the Figure 9 speech), the task is considerably
more difficult. Unless the relations are to be hopelessly garbled
in the transmission, the speaker must decompose the idea structure and arrange it into such a sequential order that the listener
will reconstitute it in essentially the same shape as it existed for
the speaker. The more complicated the idea structure he wishes
to communicate, the more difficult this job will be and the more
carefully it must be done. A major source of ineffectiveness in
communication is the inability of speakers and writers to manage this decomposition and sequential ordering in such a way
that the idea structure grown by the listener as he listens to the
speech will correspond to the idea structure intended by the
speaker.

SEGMENTAL SEQUENCE AND NESTING.

We have noted that each of the entries in an outline (and
therefore each of the circled elements in an idea structure) represents a commitment to develop a corresponding content segment. These content segments represent the manifest substance
of the speech and the greatest part of its total length. The task
of speech composition consists of developing these segments,
arranging them in an optimal sequence, and providing the additional segments that will clarify their relation to one another.

In order to understand this operation, we need to make a
distinction between simple content segments (which we will
call "simple segments") and more complex segments (which we
will call "nested segments"). The simple content segments of
Figure 9 are all of the *numbered* segments in Division 2 (the
Body or Development of the speech), except for those that are
italicized, plus Segment 2 from Division 1. These fall into three
broad categories: following traditional terminology, we will call

them "thesis," "statement of point," and "supporting details."

In a coherent speech there is only one "thesis." It is the central idea around which the idea structure is clustered. It may be what is sometimes called a "subject sentence," which presents the speech in abstract or capsule form, or a "topic sentence" which simply announces the topic of the speech. Or it may be a "purpose sentence," which is a public statement of what the speaker hopes to accomplish with the speech. Finally, it may take a more elaborate form, such as Segment 2 in Figure 9. But regardless of its specific form, a coherent discourse will contain some segment that provides a central focus for all of the ideas contained in the speech; ordinarily it will appear very close to the beginning of the speech, though often it will not be the first segment.

Most speeches of any length will contain several segments that may be characterized as "statements of points," and a long speech will contain many of them. Moreover, unless the idea structure of the speech is extremely simple, these statements will be ordered hierarchically: that is, in an outline of the speech, some will be subordinated to others. Those point statements that are subordinated directly to the thesis are usually called "statements of main points," those that are subordinated to main points are called "statements of subpoints," those that are subordinated to subpoints are called "statements of subsubpoints," and so on. It is useful to retain this terminology in order to distinguish among the various levels of subordination in the outline, and to indicate the remoteness of a given idea from the central idea of the speech. Usually a segment stating a point will be no longer than a single sentence, although point statements of two or even more sentences are not uncommon. In a speech about the small, spiderlike "false scorpions," for instance, one might state one of the main points in a single sentence as follows: "False scorpions, though common, are rarely seen because they prefer secluded habitats." Or, the same point might be stated more elaborately in two sentences: "If false scorpions are so common, you may wonder why you so seldom see one. The reason is that they prefer secluded habitats."

The "supporting details" are often developed into segments that are considerably longer than point statement segments. These supporting details take on a variety of different forms: examples and illustrations, particulars, anecdotes, facts and figures, comparisons and contrasts, quotations and authorities, and others. In a speech designed primarily to inform an audience, the supporting materials are the ideas the speaker brings to bear in order to clarify or add detail to the listener's understanding of the points. In a speech with an argumentative intent, supporting materials constitute the details of the "proof."

A nested segment is a longer segment containing two or more simple segments. Because some nested segments are more complex than others, we need a consistent terminology for distinguishing one level of complexity from another. We may preserve the necessary discriminations by referring to the *order of nesting* for a given segment, which we shall define as equivalent to the level of complexity of the point or points the segment represents: the more complex a segment, the higher its order of nesting.

A first-order idea cluster is one in which all ideas are related directly to a single idea. Of special interest in a complex idea structure are what we may call the terminal first-order clusters; "terminal" because they are the last clusters one encounters as he moves outward from the central idea. There are five terminal first-order clusters in Figure 12. Elements 13, 14, 15, and 16 constitute a terminal cluster; 18, 19, 20, and 21 constitute another; a third is represented by 4, 5, 6, and 7; a fourth is composed of 22 and 23; and the last is made up of 11 and 12. A first-order nested segment presents a terminal first-order cluster of the idea structure—a cluster of supporting details and the point of lowest subordination to which they are related.

A second-order nested segment presents two or more terminal clusters. Thus, it contains two or more first-order segments and a summarizing simple segment. A third-order segment presents two or more second-order clusters. Thus, it contains two or more second-order segments and a summarizing simple segment. The order of nesting in the speech as a whole is equal to the order of complexity of the idea structure, and this is in turn equal to the number of levels of subordination in the outline of the speech (when the outline, as in Figure 11, contains elements corresponding to the supporting materials).

It is axiomatic that a speech should reflect accurately the ideas the speaker wishes to convey to his audience and the relations among those ideas. It is for this reason that the nesting of segments in the discourse should correspond to the clustering of ideas in the idea structure; for it is the nesting in the text that will determine the idea structure that the listener grows as he listens to the speech. There are some striking similarities between message structure and idea structure. To guarantee correspondence between the speaker's idea structure and the structure of the discourse, certain features of arrangement call for special attention.

To begin with, every nested segment in a coherent discourse contains a simple segment summarizing, abstracting, or characterizing the content of that nested segment. It is toward this end that teachers of composition stress two important principles of organization: (1) subject sentence, main points, subpoints, subsubpoints, etc. should be clearly and precisely stated, and (2) each point should be stated at the place in the speech where that point is developed. Thus, in Figure 9, segment 10 is a simple segment abstracting the second-order nested segment called Point II, and both segment 4 and segment 8 are simple segments which characterize the first-order nested segment called Point I; moreover, within Point II, segment 13 is a simple segment abstracting the content of the first-order nested segment called Subpoint B. Thus, regardless of the order of nesting within it, every nested segment contains a simple segment characterizing its content.

The simple segment summarizing or abstracting a nested segment always appears in that segment for the first time either at the beginning or at the end of the nested segment. If the point statement is the first segment, then the point is said to be arranged "deductively"; if it is the last segment, then the point is said to be arranged "inductively." We shall follow this terminology because it is supported by long tradition, but the choice of words was unfortunate. "Deductive" suggests operations moving from the general to the particular; and "inductive," from the particular to the general. Sometimes the relationships among the levels of subordination in an outline will support this interpretation, but more often they will not. Referring to the subordinate-superordinate arrangement as "inductive" preserves the fiction that subpoints are somehow more specific than points, and that supporting materials are somehow more specific than subpoints, and we know that this is not the case.

Two ideas are likely to be seen as related to one another if they are presented in close temporal proximity. The greater the length of time intervening between presentation of two ideas, the smaller the likelihood that the listener will form or perceive a relationship between the two. For maximum likelihood that the listener will connect two ideas, one should be presented immediately following the other; for minimum likelihood that he will connect two ideas, they should be separated by the greatest possible number of other segments. This principle suggests that simple segments presenting ideas that are related directly to one another in the speaker's idea structure should be placed contiguously to one another in the speech; but due to the temporal sequence problem, this is seldom possible.

Consider, for instance, the idea cluster for a speech represented by Figure 15. (For now, ignore the multiple lines connecting some of the points.) The foregoing principle would suggest that E and F_1 should be presented in sequential order, and this poses no problem. However, E should be placed in immediate sequence with both F_2 and F_3 as well. The only way to

FIGURE 15
HYPOTHETICAL IDEA STRUCTURE
FOR A SPEECH

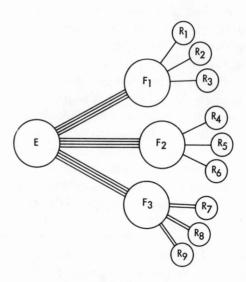

accomplish this is to repeat E three times, and this would increase redundancy beyond the point of tolerance. This implies that in a complex idea structure, the arrangement that would be ideal from the standpoint of listener comprehension of relationships is not available.

Nor does the problem in this instance stop with the first level of subordination. A typical speech plan for the idea structure of Figure 15 is represented by the outline of Figure 16. In addition to the problem already mentioned, the speaker will encounter an additional problem as he moves from the first level of subordination to the second. He cannot present R_1, R_2, and R_3 simultaneously; and unless corresponding segments are fairly short (say, not more than 30 seconds or 75 words each), it is conceivable that F_1 will have faded from awareness before R_3 is presented, so that the relation between the two will not occur

FIGURE 16
OUTLINE FOR FIGURE 15 SPEECH

E _____

F$_1$ _____

R$_1$ _____

R$_2$ _____

R$_3$ _____

F$_2$ _____

R$_4$ _____

R$_5$ _____

R$_6$ _____

F$_3$ _____

R$_7$ _____

R$_8$ _____

R$_9$ _____

without calling special attention to it. The same problem, of course, will be encountered with F_2 and F_3.

We have thus far concentrated on the way in which temporal sequencing makes it difficult to form connections between ideas; but the reverse is also true: ideas that really do not belong together may be accidentally related if one of them follows the other immediately in the speech. If the listener forms connections between ideas that are located in different branches of the speaker's idea structure, lack of comprehension or outright misunderstanding may occur. It is conceivable, for example, that the listener might mistakenly try to form some connection between R_3 and F_2, because of their immediate succession in the speech, even though in the speaker's idea structure they are not at all directly related. In the next section, we shall explore several means of overcoming both of these aspects of the temporal sequence problem.

In addition to immediate temporal proximity, speakers use a variety of specialized verbal devices to underscore and reinforce the structure of the speech. These serve not only to segment the discourse in such a way that coincidentally proximate items are separated from one another, but also to either provide or reinforce connections between segments that are related but not immediately proximate.

To illustrate these techniques for verbal reinforcement of structure, let us suppose that the speech represented by Figures 15 and 16 is a speech about some effect (E), that it discusses three factors contributing to the effect (F_1-F_3), and that three reasons are to be given why each of the factors contributes to E (R_1-R_9). After some introductory material, the speaker would ordinarily begin by presenting a segment expressing E. Now he is presented with the problem mentioned above: he cannot present F_1, F_2, and F_3 simultaneously, but it is important that all three be related to E. The speaker may at this point employ a device which we shall call *structural feed-forward*: he may tell the audience, "Three factors contribute to this effect." In doing so, he sets up anticipations in his listeners which might be described as creating a partial structure, as represented in Figure 17. Because it creates anticipations which will be fulfilled only later in the speech, this partial structure may be said to be "fed-forward" to the point where the empty dotted circles will be filled by specific content ideas.

A special form of structural feed-forward has been recognized by rhetoricians for generations; it is called the *partition*. A partition not only creates a partial structure, it also fills the empty circles of Figure 17. In this instance, a partition might read, "Three factors which contribute to this effect E are F_1, F_2, and F_3."

FIGURE 17
STRUCTURAL FEED-FORWARD
"Three factors contribute to this effect."

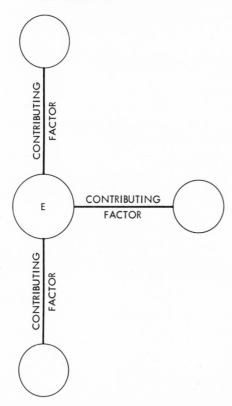

Immediately after the structural feed-forward (or partition), the speaker (following the plan of Figure 16) will move into a consideration of his first main point. To make it clear that he is doing so, he may use a *signpost transition*, perhaps coupled with the statement of the first main point. The signpost is a simple order indicator such as, "In the first place, F_1." This reinforces the connection between E and F_1, as indicated in Figure 18.

Perhaps as much as three minutes will elapse between the statement of the first main point and the statement of the second main point. In order to mark the boundary between these main points, and to increase the likelihood that R_1, R_2, and R_3 will be connected to F_1, the speaker may, after presenting the supporting ideas, *restate* F_1.

FIGURE 18
SIGNPOST TRANSITION
"In the first place, F_1 . . ."

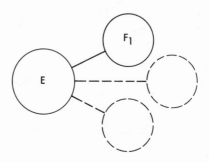

In moving on to the connection between E and F_2, the speaker may employ a second signpost transition: "The second contributing factor is F_2." As displayed in Figure 19, this signpost reinforces the relation between the thesis and the second main

FIGURE 19
SIGNPOST TRANSITION
"The second contributing factor is F_2."

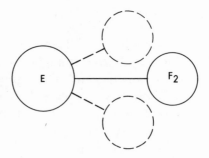

point in much the same way the earlier signpost reinforced the relation between the thesis and the first main point.

In introducing the third main point, the speaker may use another signpost transition. However, if a considerable time has elapsed since the feed-forward of the partial idea structure, and if the last point is to be developed fairly extensively, then stronger reinforcement of the entire $E–F_1–F_2–F_3$ cluster may be required. This may be provided by a *flashback-preview transition*, such as: "Not only do F_1 and F_2 contribute, but F_3 is a contributing factor also."

FIGURE 20
FLASHBACK-PREVIEW TRANSITION
"Not only do F_1 and F_2 contribute, but F_3 is a contributing factor also."

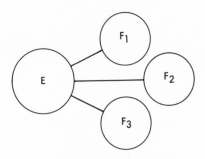

If F_3 is indeed fairly extensive, it is possible that for at least some listeners F_3 will have begun to fade from awareness by the time R_7, R_8, and R_9 have been presented. In order to reemphasize the point, the speaker may use a *partial summary*. He may even arrange it so that the partial summary reiterates the relation of F_3 to E: "Therefore, because of R_7, R_8, and R_9, F_3 contributes to E."

As a final reinforcement, if the speaker feels there may still be some listeners who are likely not to be able to remember the main points of the speech, he may use a *final summary*, which restates the thesis and the main points: "We have seen that there are three major factors that contribute to E: F_1, F_2, and F_3." This reinforces the same relationships as were reinforced earlier by the flashback-preview transition in Figure 20.

FIGURE 21

PARTIAL SUMMARY

"Therefore, because of R_7, R_8, and R_9,
F_3 contributes to E.

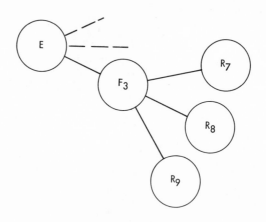

It is rare that a speech of no greater complexity than that represented by Figure 15 would require more verbal reinforcement of structure than the example discussed here; yet even in this case, a surprisingly small proportion of the total utterance will have been devoted to these transitional and other structural devices. A speech presenting thirteen different ideas, with the transitional devices mentioned here, would contain twenty-two simple segments: thirteen simple content segments, seven structural segments, and an additional segment each for introduction and conclusion. Although seven of the twenty-two segments are structural (one structural feed-forward, one flashback-preview, one restatement, one partial summary, two signpost transitions, and a final summary) , yet they are among the shortest segments in the entire speech, totaling perhaps no more than a hundred words. Estimating that a speech of this complexity would run to perhaps 2,000 words, the structural segments account for no more than 5% of the total speech length; yet this is an extremely significant 5%, which clarifies and reinforces the relations among the other segments. Moreover, it may be surprising to note the frequency with which the various relations in the speech have been reinforced by these few words. In Figure 15, the number of lines connecting each pair of ideas indicates the number of times each connection has been presented or reinforced. Each of the relations between the thesis and the main points has been reinforced four times.

The same functions may be seen in more concrete form in the Figure 9 speech. The last sentence of segment 2 contains a structural feed-forward; segment 3 is a signpost transition; segment 8 is a restatement; segment 9 is a signpost transition; segment 17 is a flashback-preview transition; segment 24 is a restatement; and segment 25 is a final summary. Because some of these segments are long, the Figure 9 speech contains an unusually high proportion of material devoted to verbal reinforcement of structure.

From the hypothetical speech of Figure 15 as well as the actual speech of Figure 9, it is clear that these structural devices play two important functions in the speech. First, they segment the discourse, increasing the likelihood that the hearer will make appropriate divisions in the content, so that ideas that are *not* immediately related do not become mixed. Second, they provide explicit instructions for connecting ideas that are so far separated in the speech that they might not be connected to one another without special effort, and they reinforce these remote connections, thus increasing the likelihood that the listener, as he hears the speech, will grow an idea structure similar to that intended by the speaker.

Introductions and Conclusions

Two of the types of simple segment we have discussed thus far occupy places of special interest in the introduction and conclusion of the speech. The thesis, though it is in fact one of the simple content segments of the nested segment that includes the body of the speech, has traditionally been viewed as an indispensable element of the introduction of the speech. In Figure 9 we have shown it as one of two introductory segments.

Segment 1, however, plays a different role entirely. It represents what has sometimes been called "interest content" or "attention material," because of the need in many speeches to provide some means of enlisting the interest and attention of the listeners at the very beginning of the speech. It is sometimes felt that the first few sentences of a speech should be especially compelling, showing why the listener should be interested in the topic, or why it is important, or why he should listen to the speech; they should answer the question, "so what?"

Perhaps the most general way of describing the type of introductory material in segment 1 is that it is designed to relate the thesis (and therefore the whole content of the speech) to things outside the speech. By connecting the speech to experiences, values, issues, or concepts that are important or valuable or interesting, a motivation is created for listening and a frame of reference is established which will enhance recall and effective utilization of the speech content on future occasions. Therefore, it is not enough that the material be simply interesting and relevant to the thesis; it must locate the speech with respect to ideas that the listener presumably already has. It must establish a context for the speech.

Sometimes material like that in segment 1 is not only superfluous but is in fact exceedingly irritating. This happens when a context for the speech has already been created by others or by circumstances before the speech begins. In a congressional debate, for instance, such "attention" material is generally out of place, as it is whenever previous speakers or the context of the situation has given the audience reasonably complete and accurate anticipations about what, in general, the speaker will talk. Thus, not all speeches require orienting or attention material in the introduction. Often a simple statement of the thesis is all that the situation will bear.

Nor will all speeches require an elegant conclusion. Tradition assigns the final summary to the conclusion (as segment 25 in Figure 9) rather than including it as a part of the body of the speech. If the speech has been long, or has displayed a complex idea structure, a summary generally is desirable as a means of reinforcing idea relations; but if it is not required for that purpose, then it certainly is not necessary merely to end the speech.

It is argued sometimes that a conclusion should terminate the speech on a strong note or in a definite way so that the audience senses that the speech is over. This sort of conclusion is required especially on formal occasions, because audiences are more likely to expect such a conclusion then. It may be inappropriate in an informal gathering, or when one is speaking on a panel and is to be followed immediately by other speakers. But where it is not inappropriate, a strong conclusion does much to support the remembered effectiveness of the speech and can serve to enhance the general image of the speaker. The effect in question can be obtained by concluding with an imaginative restatement of the thesis, or by including materials that, like those in the "attention" segment of the introduction, place the speech in a larger context. Segment 26 contains materials that perform both of these functions.

Assignment: A Rhetorical Jigsaw Puzzle

When put in their proper sequence, the phrases, sentences, and paragraphs of the following exercise form a well-organized speech. Each "bit" or segment can be identified as a certain kind of speech segment, such as Introductory Attention Material, Transition, Example, Statement of Subpoint, Summary, etc. (Some segments may be classified in more than one way.)

Copy each of these segments onto a separate slip of paper. Rearrange the order of segments until you are satisfied that you have the best possible speech that can be made using all of these segments (and only these segments). After you have the speech arranged, classify each of the segments according to the type of content it represents.

Finally, make an outline of the body of the speech only, showing subject or purpose sentence, main point (s), subpoint (s), and type (s) of supporting material used, as in Figure 10.

Take for instance this desk. As a tree it had no value other than the pleasure derived from its shade. But the minute it was cut down, sawed into boards and assembled into a desk, it became valuable. The fact that human labor made a desk from a tree made this wood—this desk—valuable.

In this happy society there will be no force, no struggle. We will all be absolutely free and absolutely equal, and we'll all receive absolute justice. Each of us will give according to his abilities and each of us will receive according to his needs. It is a land sweet with honey and full of human kindness.

The idea of capitalist exploitation arises from the question: If labor creates value, how come the capitalist gets profit on a product made from the efforts of labor?

The Labor Theory of Value was one of Marx's main ideas in regard to capitalist states.

But after the collapse of capitalism—what then? The prophet Marx foretells the blissful life we will all lead under the great communist states.

"The centralization of the means of production and socialization of labour," says Marx, "reach a point where they prove incompatible with their capitalist husk. This bursts asunder. The knell of capitalist private property sounds. The expropriators are expropriated. . . . With the inexorability of a law of nature, capitalist production begets its own negation."

Again, let us return to this desk.

Marx reasoned that the capitalists, by keeping profit, are robbing the workers of their just due.

Well now—from the labor theory of value, the idea of capitalist exploitation follows.

In this concept, he maintains that a good or item is valuable because of the labor that goes into its creation, and only labor can make things valuable.

According to Marx, capitalism will collapse of its own weight.

Therefore, you see, labor and human labor alone has injected value into this desk. This basically is the labor theory of value.

What Marx is saying is that capitalism will go through a series of depressions and recoveries with capitalistic monopoly of a few super wealthy people and a great number of depressed workers emerging after each cycle of depression and recovery. All competition will end, and a sort of finance monopoly will reign. At this point the antagonism between capitalist and proletariat will be so great that something will have to crack. Marx says the capitalist husk—meaning the capitalist economic system —will crack, because the workers will revolt and seize the means of production.

By now, you're probably asking yourself the same questions that Marx asked himself, and maybe you're coming up with the same answers.

Somehow it seems a shame that he was so horribly wrong.

About sixty-five years ago, on Saint Patrick's Day, a German exile living in London was buried. Eighteen-eighty-three was the exact year, but before he died, Karl Marx calculated and published his concept of Scientific Socialism. Contrary to popular opinion, socialism had existed before Marx, but it had been of an undisciplined, utopian variety. Marx tried to show scientifically what was wrong with capitalism, why it must fail, and what would happen when it did.

I have covered two aspects of Marxian economics: the Labor Theory of Value and Capitalist Exploitation. But Marx did not stop there. With this economic crystal ball, made of labor value and based on the class struggle, he foretold first the doom of capitalism, and second the idyllic life that he expected to follow the establishment of the great communist states.

Because so few of us understand what Marx really intended, I'd like to review some of the basic ideas of Marxian Socialism.

The labor which invested this hunk of wood with value may have been fairly well paid. But certainly the price the University paid for it amounted to more than the sum total of the wages of the men who made and sold it. Fifty cents here and a dollar there went into the pockets of men who did nothing but own the buildings, land, and machines that the workers used to produce it.

Speech Preparation Assignment

In the next speech you prepare for classroom presentation, prepare the following to show to your instructor on the class day before you are to deliver the speech:

1. A full outline of the speech (either a sentence outline or a topic outline) with supporting materials indicated by type (but not reproduced in full). See Figure 10.

2. A representation of the idea structure of the speech, in the fashion of Figure 12. This diagram should represent the body of the speech only (do not include the introduction or conclusion).

3. A full text of the proposed speech, divided into organizational segments, in the fashion of Figure 9. Underline transitions, and by means of nested brackets such as those used in Figure 9, show the nesting of content segments in the speech. In the margin, identify each content segment according to its function in the speech (classify it according to the type of segment it represents).

(This is likely to prove a particularly demanding assignment. It provides an excellent opportunity for small peer groups of students working together to check one another's analysis, and for intensive individual work in faculty-student conferences.)

chapter 5

ANALYSIS OF

AUDIENCE

AND OCCASION:

THE IMMEDIATE

SOCIAL CONTEXT

We have so far presented a point of view for the study of speech communication and discussed a broad strategy for communication in social action. We also have examined some functions of the speaker as he approaches the task of speech preparation, and explored the macrostructure of speeches. Frequently we have found the listener to be a touchstone for evaluating principles and distinguishing among situations; however, up to now he has occupied a subsidiary position in our analysis.

In this and the next chapter, however, we turn our attention directly upon the listener. Rhetoric has been characterized as the art of fitting ideas to people and people to ideas.[1] To do so properly, one must know something about the people to whom the ideas are to be fitted. Audience analysis undertakes this job in a particular setting. Its ultimate goal is to determine what kind of message (if any) will be most likely to achieve a given purpose with a particular audience; but, first it looks at the characteristics of the listeners and the speaking situation.

In exploring audience analysis in these two chapters, we do not concentrate primarily on achieving a particular purpose, but rather on becoming sensitive to certain aspects of listener and situation that make a particular difference in response to communication. The present chapter approaches the matter from the standpoint of several general aspects of audience and occasion which are often important in planning for communication; Chapter 6 deals with one specific, but extremely pervasive, factor of audience behavior and response.

[1]Donald C. Bryant and Karl R. Wallace, *Fundamentals of Public Speaking*, 3rd edition (New York: Appleton-Century-Crofts, 1953), p. 3.

WHY ANALYZE THE AUDIENCE?

The need for audience analysis arises from a desire to calculate the probable effects of a speech. Because audiences differ in background, experiences, and interests, no two of them will react in exactly the same way to any given message; and to achieve a similar effect with two different audiences may require two quite different messages. Therefore, any use of public speaking as an instrument of social action requires that we take into consideration differences in the audience which may shape the immediate and/or long-range effects of a speech.

In one sense, much of this book has been concerned with audience analysis; for it has dealt with the consequences (in terms of audience response) of various courses of action on the part of the speaker. However, most of this information has dealt with audiences *in general*; this chapter deals with differences between *particular* audiences which may change the way in which many principles operate or may introduce altogether new considerations. These differences are important because they are reflections of the context in which the speech is made and received. The auditor is not like a blank slate upon which the ideas of the speaker may be written at will; whom he perceives himself to be and what he perceives himself to be doing at the time of the speech are matters that have profound effect upon what the speech means to him.

IS AUDIENCE ANALYSIS POSSIBLE?

Granted that audience analysis is desirable, the next question that arises is whether it is possible. In fact, the question arises from the same considerations that prompt us to consider audience analysis in the first place. We claim a need for audience analysis on the ground that audiences differ; yet, if we carry the analysis further we find that individual auditors within the same audience differ from one another as much as one audience differs from another.

The concept of "the audience" is, after all, merely an abstraction. No such creature exists. The ultimate reality in every case is the individual auditor; and if we attribute to the audience as a whole the average or typical or representative characteristics of the individuals who compose it, are we not making as great a mistake as we would in assuming that all audiences are the same? In the final analysis it is the individual auditors (not some hypothetical totality called "the audience") who will receive and respond to our message. In that case, should we not speak of "auditor analysis" and tailor a different speech for each member of the audience? And since this is impossible, are we not deluding ourselves with the notion of audience analysis for *public* speaking?

This question is not trivial, for every feature of our communicative lives bears testimony to the important fact that auditors differ. What teacher would not prefer tutoring a single student to lecturing fifty? What salesman does not prefer to talk to his clients one at a time? Does not the priest witness greater spiritual growth in individual counseling sessions than in regular mass services? Are not door-to-door ward workers an indispensible cog in every political machine? With a few important exceptions (to be noted later) communication with individuals is more effective than communication with groups. That is, the speaker is more likely to accomplish more of what he sets out to do when the circumstances permit him to talk with people one at a time, because the give-and-take of conversation provides him opportunity to perform detailed auditor analysis and to adapt his message to the individual.

In view of these considerations the question is not whether audiences differ, but whether the individual members of a given audience have enough in common with one another to warrant a speaker's efforts to adapt his message to their common characteristics. This question can in turn be reduced to two further questions:

(1) To what extent are the members of an audience likely to be similar to one another?

(2) Are their similarities important in determining whether alternative forms of the message contemplated by the speaker will differ in their effects upon the audience?

Audience analysis may be used with profit only if both of these questions can be answered "yes."

Let us perform an imaginary experiment. Suppose that from the telephone book of a medium-sized American town we select one phone number at random from every fifth page, giving us a total of, let us say, 100 numbers. Suppose we then call each of these numbers and ask the person who answers the telephone to appear at a predetermined time to listen to a speech. If all 100 persons show up, we shall have a nearly random (technically an "accidental") collection of individuals who are likely to be very different from one another. They will probably range from very old to very young, from well-off to poor, from unschooled to well-educated. There will be Democrats and Republicans; Catholics, Jews, and several varieties of Protestants; people of various racial and ethnic backgrounds; men and women; the representatives of various professions and occupations, as well as the unemployed. Yet even these people—widely different as they would be—have two things in common: Each of them is a member of a household that owns at least one listed telephone, and each was willing and able to come to participate in the experiment.

Moreover, on the basis of these two bits of information we may perhaps infer more, even before our audience assembles. In the first place, we can predict that the audience probably will not include very young children or the aged and infirm, since parental refusal in the first case and physical inability in the second would likely prevent their attendance. Nor would our audience be likely to include either the destitute (who could not afford a telephone) or the enormously rich (who generally don't list their private numbers in the public directory). The student may find it amusing to speculate about other traits that may be inferred in turn from these bits of information.

Of course, we need to keep in mind that only the first two bits of information are *known*; everything else in *inferred*, and these inferences may be mistaken. A four-year-old may show up with a parent in tow; a palsied octogenarian may be brought in on a stretcher; we may have called the one pauper in town who spends everything on a telephone or the one millionnaire with a listed phone. But it is highly probable that our audience will not contain persons of these types. In a very loose sense, then, our auditors may be said to have something in common with one another.

Moreover, after the experiment gets underway they will have still more in common—namely, the accumulating experience of the experimental setting and stimuli themselves; the instructions, tests, and experimental messages that are involved in completing the experiment. They now have a (limited) background of common experience, which grows continually as the experiment progresses, so that at the end of the experimental session they are more like one another in some respects than they were at the beginning. If we now convene this same group on some later occasion for another phase of our experiment, we shall not be surprised to find them noticeably more alike at the beginning of the second session than they were at the outset of the first.

SOURCES OF HOMOGENEITY

Of course the procedure we have outlined here is an extremely unlikely method of creating an audience. The usual procedure is quite different. More often than not, the audience is some more or less permanent group which assembles regularly for stated purposes. Speakers come and go but the group tends to remain constant, and its members tend to have a good deal in common with one another. An individual is likely to be selected for membership in such a group on the basis of his similarity to, or compatibility with, others already in membership, and once in the group he tends to become still more like his fellow members because within the confines of the group he is exposed to the same things they are. Thus the members of any permanent group tend to have vastly more in common with one another than do members of a transitory group assembled at random from the telephone book.

Even when the members of an audience are not members of the same permanent group (lodge, religious congregation, service club, professional association, legislature, trade union, alumni group, etc.) they are almost always assembled for some specific purpose, which is intimately related to what the speaker hopes to accomplish. Often they are assembled especially to listen to speeches on a particular topic. Such a collection of individuals is not random; each has some reason for being there which involves some kind of commitment to the speaker, the topic under discussion, or other members of the audience. On these occasions too, as in permanent groups, there are strong forces toward homogeneity within the audience.

We have seen that even when an audience is selected in an apparently haphazard and artificial way its members are likely to have at least a few traits in common and that the actual audiences that speakers face tend to have much in common with respect to general traits, experiences, and purposes. However, the question remains whether these similarities are such as might make a difference to the speaker insofar as his purposes are concerned. It is one thing to say that the members of an audience are similar in certain ways; it is quite another to say that these similarities will affect their response to what the speaker has to say.

Thus far we have noted two sources of similarity among members of natural groups: (1) an individual tends to join groups whose members are similar to or compatible with himself; and (2) once in a group, all members tend to become more alike because they are exposed to the same influences. Both of these forces tend to make individuals more predictable in their behavior. In most speaking situations a knowledge of these two factors—that is, what the group members have in common and what they do in the group—will prove a rich source of insights concerning what will interest the group members, what the speaker's ideas will mean to them, and what symbols may serve as common bases of persuasion.

It may generally be said that most natural audiences are composed of individuals who have enough traits and experiences in common to serve as bases of interest, understanding, and acceptance for a wide variety of topics. Through judicious inquiry and forethought the speaker may find it possible to locate those common traits and experiences that can be brought to bear on his topic and purpose. However, these useful commonalities may not come to light readily; for there is no list of traits and/or experiences that are universally useful in audience analysis, and there is probably no human trait or experience that might not be useful with respect to some topic or other. What the speaker requires for intelligent and efficient audience analysis is some search principle that may help him to discover useful properties of the audience while saving him the necessity of checking through an infinitely long list of human attributes.

In our discussion of audience analysis and adaptation, we will develop two such search principles. In this chapter, we shall explore a series of five questions designed to lead to useful information about auditors. In Chapter 6, we shall raise questions about the roles the auditor plays both in the speech situation and in the larger context in which the speaker hopes to achieve influence, and about the way in which these roles modify and shape his response to communication.

INFLUENCE OF KNOWLEDGE ABOUT AUDITORS

In general, characteristics of the audience and occasion exert four main kinds of influence on the speaker. First, they establish *restraints*—things "not allowed." It is rarely appropriate to use humor in a funeral oration, or at the dedication of a monument, or in arguing for the passage of major legislation. When we say that such behaviors are not permitted, we do not mean that they are never done; but simply that when they are done, the speaker is likely to be misunderstood, regarded with disapproval, and largely ineffectual. The audience and occasion set limits to what can be done effectively, and consideration of audience characteristics helps to define the limits of effective communication.

Second, audience characteristics establish *constraints*—things "required." For instance, when speaking to people with no background in your subject, it is regarded as essential to provide them with some explanation of the relevance of the topic to their interests and concerns. Or, when using unfamiliar technical terms, one is constrained to define them as they are introduced. This is not to say that it is utterly impossible to speak on such occasions without doing these things, but if these amenities are omitted, they are sure to be missed and the impact of the speech will be severely reduced.

Third, characteristics of the audience and occasion provide *criteria for selecting among alternate forms of the message.* Suppose, for example, that one were designing a speech to be presented at alumni dinners as part of a college fund-raising campaign, and that all of the major appeals have been worked out except one. Suppose that in developing the point that contributions are needed to support research, time limitations make it necessary to choose *either* an appeal based on the value of research in advancing man's knowledge *or* an appeal based on the importance of research in building the prestige and academic standing of the institution. Knowing that the speech will be presented at several alumni dinners, one is able to apply a firm criterion for selecting between the two possible appeals. Although a given alumni group on a particular occasion might respond more favorably to the first argument, the one role that all auditors will be playing on such occasions is the role of The Old Grad; and the argument based on the value of research to the prestige and standing of their alma mater is likely to be more effective than the generalized appeal to the value of increased knowledge to mankind at large. The dominant audience role provides a criterion for selecting the most appropriate argument. Similar criteria apply to selecting supporting details, testimony, statistics, and even the language in which ideas are expressed.

Fourth, occasion and audience characteristics suggest *opportunities for producing special effects*. Imagine a speaker who is to deliver a speech on "The Information Explosion" at a city chamber of commerce luncheon. Knowing that his audience will be composed largely of businessmen, the speaker may be motivated to consider the question, "How has the information explosion affected and been affected by business?" Prompted by this question, the speaker may discover that entirely new businesses and industries have been created by demands for abstracting services, information retrieval systems, and other outgrowths of the information explosion. This information in turn, may lead the speaker to discover particularly appropriate specific purposes, to add or substitute new main points, to include certain lines of development, or to add supporting examples or comparisons. In short, this question, suggested by the special nature of his audience, may direct the speaker's attention into particular areas of his over-all topic that could be especially interesting, valuable, and effective for the specific audience he will face.

SOME PRODUCTIVE QUESTIONS
ABOUT AUDIENCE AND OCCASION

It is one thing to know that the four types of influence just discussed can operate, and quite another to know how to bring them into operation in formulating a message for a particular audience. Because the identification of restraints, constraints, decision principles, and special opportunities involves a number of factors that interact in a complex way, applied audience analysis is regarded as something of an art. It is not now possible to reduce the art to a rigorous scientific basis, but it is possible to identify certain questions as logical starting points for analysis. These questions will not direct the speaker unerringly to proper decisions about speech content, but they will point him toward lines of inquiry which are likely to yield useful information. If the speaker then follows through on the leads these questions provide, if he is sensitive and knowledgeable enough to understand the significance of what he finds, and if he has the creative talent to adapt his message accordingly, he is almost certain to produce greater impact through his speeches. Even if he does not, answers to the questions will enable him to predict more accurately the probable effects of whatever speech he does produce.

1. *What is the activation level of the audience?* "Activation" refers to general arousal level. After a meal, or early in the morning, or after strenuous exercise, or at the end of a long program of speeches, the activation level of the ordinary auditor is likely to be near low ebb. This state of affairs has a physiological basis; the listener's respiration, heart rate, and other organic processes are depressed when the activation level is low, and elevated when activation level is high—indeed, physiological arousal is one of the more reliable indices of activation. But the physiological state is accompanied by and interacts with the listener's psychological condition. An activated listener is more excited (and excitable), more alert, more receptive, and more discriminating. He can pay close attention, consume information at a faster rate, and respond more quickly and more deeply than the deactivated listener.

To achieve a given level of response will require stronger stimulation for the deactivated listener than would be required for the activated listener. In Chapter 7, we will note that adaptations of loudness, rate, vocal variety, and other aspects of delivery may be required to compensate for deactivation. Insofar as content is concerned, it is usually pointless to undertake detailed explanations or complex chains of reasoning with such listeners. If any response is to be obtained at all, it will be through variety, change of pace, and speech materials that have high interest and motivational value. With such auditors, special attention to factors of clarity is required. If the material is clear and forceful, interesting and highly motivating, and presented energetically, the deactivated listener may be at least partially reactivated during the speech.

Although we can depend upon the deactivated listener to be initially unreceptive, we cannot be sure that increasing levels of activation will invariably lead to increasing receptiveness. Much depends upon both the degree and the source of activation. Extremely high levels of activation are characterized by high emotion; under the influence of strong emotion, the listener will be quite unreceptive to subtleties and shades of difference, and quite intolerant of opposing points of view. He will be inclined to see things in bold contrasts, to be impatient with rationalization, and to overrespond to favorable images and arguments.

Quite a different problem is presented by the audience whose high activation arises from factors that are extrinsic to the speech. Usually this kind of hyperactivation is not predictable far in advance; the speaker discovers this condition in his audience just prior to speaking. Under such circumstances, unless he is to lose the audience altogether, the speaker will have to take them where he finds them and meet them at their own level. For example, a speaker who is scheduled to talk in a speech class following a very exciting previous speaker will ordinarily not be able to proceed with his own talk exactly as he planned it. If he can find a link between the preceding speech topic and his own, he may be able to capitalize on the connection; but in any case, he will have to say something about the preceding speech before proceeding with his own. A comparable situation occurs quite often at conventions, political rallies, and service club programs.

Most speeches are prepared for audiences that are assumed to be neither deactivated nor hyperactivated, and whose activation level is related in part at least to moderate interest and involvement in the topic of the speech. But because most speeches are designed for such audiences, there is particular danger that the speaker will overlook the exceptional cases where these ideal circumstances do not prevail; caught off guard, he is likely to miss the mark without quite understanding why. By the same token (and particularly if he is a student in a speech course), he is likely to try to criticize speeches made by others under unusual conditions of activation *as if* they had been delivered under ideal conditions. What may seem to the student like a remarkably trivial address by a well-known civic club speaker may turn out to have been the most profound utterance that could have been delivered with any prospect of being heard by a deactivated after-dinner gathering at 7:30 on a Friday evening.

2. *What purposes are practical for this audience?* One view of speechmaking holds that, like medicine, rhetoric is to be judged by the quality of the practice rather than the nature of the outcome. In the normal course of events, members of a bereaved family do not curse the doctor who attended the deceased during his terminal illness; the usual outlook is that the doctor did all that could be done in the face of an inevitable situation, and indeed may have practiced brilliantly, though the patient died. A similar view of public speaking would allow us to applaud a speaker who practices brilliantly, even though his speech fails to achieve its manifest purpose. As you may recall from Chapter 1, a communication outlook is inconsistent with this viewpoint. To view speech as communication is to place responsibility for the outcome on the speaker rather than on the situation, any powerful opposing forces, or the audience. In particular, the speaker must understand the social context of the speech, and must adapt to it.

Perhaps the most overlooked form of audience adaptation is adjustment of the speaker's purpose (s) to the limits of the possible in a given situation. Much has already been accomplished if the speaker recognizes the possibility, on the one hand, that the goal he would most like to accomplish might be beyond the limits of practicality, or, on the other hand, that his initial purpose fails to exploit to the fullest the possibilities of a given audience situation. A speaker's total effort must be evaluated partly in terms of how well he judges the practical limits to what can be accomplished, and how wisely he adjusts his own purposes accordingly.

We use the term "practical limits" advisedly because, while one might be reluctant to admit that any goal was "impossible," given enough time and resources, it certainly is not a defeatist position to admit that in any speaking situation there exist practical limits to what can be accomplished. A very common error is to set goals that exceed these practical limits, and to avoid this error it helps to bear in mind some of the origins for such practical limits.

One source of limitation on the speaker's purpose has been noted above: the activation level of the audience. If the audience is highly activated with respect to some extrinsic source of stimulation, or is deactivated, then the speaker will have to invest more time and effort to achieve a given level of response; in practice, this may mean that the speaker will need to settle for a response that is easier to obtain than the one he most desires.

A second source of practical limits will be discussed below when we come to taboos and formal requirements. For the moment, we may note that certain kinds of purposes are held to be out of place in certain types of social situations.

A third source of limit to purpose is knowledge and experience of the auditors relative to the speaker's topic. If the audience knows little or nothing about the topic, then the speaker may have to spend considerable time providing them with concepts, information, or vicarious experiences through examples, comparisons, and other supporting materials. Because no speaker can hold an audience for an unlimited length of time, the speaker may find that he can achieve a thorough coverage of only part of what he would like to impart to the audience; and under these conditions he is well advised to scale down his purpose to accord with the knowledge and experience level of his audience and the limit of time available. This point, too, will be discussed in greater detail below.

A fourth source of limitation on the speaker's purpose is existing attitudes, values, and beliefs in the audience. An audience that is strongly opposed to abolishing capital punishment is not likely to be switched to support of abolition in a single speech. In addressing such an audience, the speaker may set as his goal providing information that will lay a groundwork for future attitude change, or moderating the audience's opposition to abolition.

Speakers err not only in setting goals that exceed the practical limitations of the situation, but also in setting goals that are so limited in terms of existing audience conditions as to make the effort of speaking scarcely worthwhile. Sometimes a speaker may expend considerable effort "beating a dead horse" when, with the investment of only slightly more effort, he might have accomplished something of value. For example, one still hears a speech occasionally in a public-speaking class on the case for a link between cigarette smoking and lung cancer. For the most part, such speeches are an exercise in futility; almost everybody in the audience already believes that such a link exists, and to elaborate the proof for a proposition that already has high credibility is generally not a wise use of speaker or audience time. Ordinarily the speaker who advances such proof is ultimately interested in getting people to quit smoking or to resist taking up the habit; and most people do not fail to engage in these behaviors out of any disbelief in the evidence for a connection between smoking and disease. On the contrary, they either do not know how to quit smoking, or they have never directly faced the issue. A speech designed to show the listener one or more useful approaches to breaking the habit, or one designed to confront him with the issue and urge an immediate decision would certainly accomplish more than a rehash of familiar arguments and evidence.

We have observed that speakers may set goals that are beyond the limits of practicality or may set goals that fall far short of the audience's readiness to respond; a third kind of error is failure to specify purpose clearly in terms of audience response. Student speakers in class sometimes deliver strong arguments in favor of pending congressional bills, without ever specifying either to their auditors or to themselves just what they hoped to accomplish by the speech in terms of specific audience behavior. We gain some insight into these speeches if we consider them from the standpoint of the limits of practicality. On one hand, the students in the class clearly are not in a position to vote on the bill, so it is inappropriate to address them as if they were congressmen or senators. On the other hand, they may be ready to do something more than simply give silent assent to the speaker's arguments. Considered from the standpoint of social action, what is it *possible* for these auditors to do? And which of the possible actions is the speaker likely to be able to get them to do through the medium of a short classroom speech? As we can see in this example, to discuss the possible is sometimes to sharpen one's own sense of purpose.

3. *What taboos and formal requirements must be observed?* It is useful to examine the nature of the audience and occasion before completing preparation of the speech, to determine whether constraints have been observed and to make sure that no restraints have been violated.

Taboos arise in part from who the speaker and listeners are. By and large, for example (at the time of this writing), it is held to be improper for men to use profanity in public situations where women are present. Many regard this taboo as a quaint, old-fashioned imperative, and some feel that it reflects outgrown values and should be abandoned. Perhaps in time it will be; but the man who violates this Victorian taboo nowadays does so at the risk of undermining his own effectiveness. Occasionally a speaker in a public-speaking class decides to try this principle, and the attempt almost invariably ends in disaster. The lesson taught by these experiences is that what constitutes an effective taboo depends not on the speaker's attitudes and habits, but upon those of the audience.

Taboos cover not only language, but also the permissible range of topics and purposes. Ordinarily it would not be wise to try to persuade people to register Republican in a valedictory address, to buy encyclopedias at a political rally, or to dedicate their lives to more worthwhile goals at a medical convention. Many of the proprieties that govern such matters are not limited to public speaking; they grow out of more general social considerations. We do not think it acceptable to introduce partisan politics into nonpartisan, apolitical ceremonial functions because the divisiveness they cause would conflict with the central function of the ceremonial occasion—to induce harmony and promote the sharing of common symbolic experiences; we regard it as poor taste to intrude personal interests into concerted political group activity, because the individual who does so draws attention and time away from the common political goals that provide the *raison d'être* of the political gathering; we object to the introduction of broad philosophical or social issues into work conferences because they dissipate the common focus on the practical considerations that brought the conferees together in the first place and that provides the major source of cohesiveness in the group.

In addition to taboos, the speaker should attend to the formal requirements of the situation: what will the audience expect of any speaker addressing them in this context? Like taboos, such formal requirements may apply to *any* aspect of the speech. For example, students frequently are taught that it is poor form to read a speech from a manuscript. In order to preserve an atmos-

phere of direct person-to-person communication in the classroom, manuscripts are regarded as taboo. Such speakers may be
confused later on when approaching audiences in other than
classroom settings; for in many such situations, a manuscript is
expected—the speaker who comes to the platform without one
may be suspected of not having done his homework thoroughly
enough, and this in turn may be taken as evidence of an improper regard for the audience. At most professional conventions, for example (including the conventions of the Speech
Association of America), the normal expectation is that research
reports and important speeches will be read from manuscript.

Sometimes a speaker feels that if he is to accomplish any purpose that he considers worthwhile, he must violate taboos or
formal requirements. Usually this opinion results from an im-
mature analysis of the situation, but occasionally it is a valid
assessment. On these occasions the speaker finds himself in a
situation of high risk. He should do whatever is possible to minimize the ill effects of violating audience expectations, and he
should be prepared to accept at least some unpleasant side
effects, if not the failure to achieve any immediate purpose with
the audience involved.

4. *What other groups are relevant to the auditors' response to
this speech?* Both daily experience and laboratory research show
that our judgments of everything, be it the quality of a painting
or the length of a line, are subject to social influence. Listeners,
too, tend to adjust their perceptions, their evaluations, their
reasoning, and their overt responses to those of the people
around them. An individual member of an audience is influenced strongly by the responses of his fellow auditors; indeed,
in many speeches, if not most, more persuasion takes place
through such social facilitation than through direct response to
the speech itself.

However, response is not limited to the observed reactions of
those who are present at the speech. A listener seldom hears a
speech through his own ear alone; particularly if the message is

in any way controversial, he is likely to check his own tentative reactions against what he imagines to be the reactions of groups who are not present but whose relation to him he feels may be influenced by his response to the speech. Such groups may be called "relevant reference groups."

Some such reference groups are formal organizations and can be identified by the speaker in advance. For instance, religious, political, and professional organizations all serve as reference groups for certain ranges of ideas. When a speaker employs ideas that are consonant with those of such a reference group, the listener finds it easier to accept what the speaker has to say than when the speaker's ideas are at odds with those of the reference group.

On the other hand, a group can also sometimes serve as a negative point of reference, so that ideas that are shown to be at variance with those of such a negative reference group are thereby made more attractive. In every generation one hears a good deal about young people "rebelling against adult authority." This rebellion is not simply the development of independent values and beliefs, but grows at least in part out of a tendency to reject whatever is associated with established ways of thinking. "People over thirty" then become a negative reference group, and a speaker who can associate any idea with this group lays a foundation for discrediting that idea. To show that a proposal is actively disapproved by the negative reference group renders that proposal potentially more appealing.

As the foregoing example shows, reference groups may be informal, and even rather vaguely defined. "Parents," "teenagers," "the Jet Set," and "ultraconservatives" are informal groupings whose membership is vaguely delineated and constantly shifting; but they are nevertheless basic reference groups for certain ranges of ideas among people who belong to, or identify with, or regulate some portion of their thinking or behavior with reference to these groups. Of particular relevance are face-to-face groups such as the neighborhood gang or the family or the car pool. Attitudes and beliefs within such groups tend to be homogeneous and extremely stable.

Almost anything a speaker says is likely to be revelant to the attitudes, beliefs, or expectations of some reference group for at least some member of the audience, and it is often the case that a speaker's major proposition asks the majority of listeners for some reaction that is relevant to a particular reference group. For example, in presenting the advantages of increased medicare benefits to a group consisting largely of physicians, the listener will be concerned not only with his own immediate reactions and evaluations, but with the responses to his reactions by other physicians he knows and by the county and state medical associations, and with the position of the AMA. It may well be that his anticipations of the responses of these relevant reference groups will play a larger part in his response than anything the speaker can say.

The speaker is, then, well advised to consider what reference groups will be relevant to the auditors' response to his speech. If their anticipated reactions are consonant with his purpose, he can use them to good advantage; if they are not, then he needs to consider whether anything can be done to moderate their influence. We shall have more to say about reference groups in the next chapter.

5. *What conventional beliefs and values will apply?* In the American Legion, patriotic duty is held in high regard; education is highly valued by the PTA; considerable worth is placed on research by the American Association for the Advancement of Science. All of the foregoing are examples of conventional values that are associated with particular groups. This is not to say that *every* member of such groups will in fact place an equally high value on these things; but at meetings of such groups, members will behave *as if* they valued these things, and appeals based on these values will carry considerable weight. These are the values that the group will not be inclined to argue or to question; some set of such values may be found in

any natural group, large or small, formal or informal. The speaker who has given some thought to these values is in a better position to formulate and to select appeals and speech materials than the speaker who knows nothing of the conventional values of the group.

In addition to values, most groups also share conventional beliefs. Members of the Ku Klux Klan, for example, profess to believe that Negroes are congenitally inferior to Caucasians in intellectual capacity. Whether a particular member holds this belief in fact may be relatively unimportant in determining response to persuasive messages directed to the Klan: the fact is that this proposition is held as a conventional belief by the group; members expect one another to behave *as if* they believed it to be true. Such conventional beliefs characterize groups of all kinds. It is important for the speaker to locate these conventional beliefs. If they are consonant with his purposes, they provide excellent grounds for his appeals; if they are at odds with his purposes, he needs to decide whether to ignore them or make a direct frontal attack on them. In any case, he will be in a better position to predict the effects of the speech if he can identify ways in which these beliefs interact with his proposed message.

6. *What factors will operate to affect the long-range outcome of the speech?* Some speeches, such as ceremonial addresses, are designed to have their principal impact at the time of delivery. Others, such as sales talks, are expected to have their principal outcome immediately following the speech. In most plans of social action, however, speeches are prepared with long-range effects in mind; even those speeches whose immediate goal is some effect in the speaking situation itself are planned so as to maximize long-term gains and minimize unfavorable long-range side effects.

Some of the factors that will affect the long-range outcome of the speech may be identified as characteristics of the auditors or the occasion. Certainly the relevant reference groups referred to above will operate in this way. As we shall see in greater detail in the next chapter, if the speaker can predict that the auditor will be reinforced in one or more of the roles he plays through adopting the belief, value, attitude, or behavior that the speaker wishes to recommend, then he can predict that any effect produced by the speech will be strengthened long afterwards through the auditor's continuing contact with his circle of acquaintances. If, on the other hand, the proposed attitude or behavior will be disapproved by members of the listener's immediate circle, then whatever the speaker might be able to accomplish during the speech is likely to be short-lived.

An everyday example of this sort of influence may be seen in the work of the speech therapist, the psychotherapist, and the marriage counselor. These professionals work diligently with individuals, trying to modify their ways of perceiving others, their attitudes and values, their beliefs, and their behavior. In a way, they are engaged in small-scale, intensive social action programs. Often, however, they find their efforts blocked by circumstances beyond their immediate control; for whatever the therapist is able to accomplish in a few hours a month is sometimes eradicated by the steady counterinfluence of groups within which the client must live his daily life.

For instance, speech therapists and teachers of speech improvement recognize a "substandard" dialect as a major challenge, and an extremely difficult problem if the student continues to live in the same community and associate with the same groups as those in which he originally developed his speech patterns. What the therapist identifies as "improved" speech will be regarded as "uppity" or "talking quality"— distinctly outgroup behavior—by many members of the client's immediate social circle. In order to minimize these effects, the therapist may counsel with the client's parents, family, employer, and friends; but in the final analysis the student will face a choice between what the teacher identifies as "good speech" and the continued good will of his primary reference groups.

If he is clever, he may become a two-dialect speaker, able to switch from what the teacher identifies as "good" speech to what the neighborhood identifies as "regular" speech and back again, depending on his surroundings. This is particularly likely to happen if the student has some situations outside the clinic or classroom where use of the "good" dialect is reinforced by others. But in the absence of such reinforcing contacts, what usually happens is that the student rejects his instruction and reverts to the patterns that provide him maximum reinforcement and minimum punishment in the groups with which he has to deal day in and day out.

What is true of changing dialect patterns is equally true of changing thought, attitudinal, and behavior patterns. If you can predict that your proposed way of thinking, believing, feeling, or behaving will provide your auditor with reinforcement in his immediate social context, or if you can provide him with a new and different context in which such reinforcement can be found, then you can predict that he will adopt what you recommend, and perhaps build upon it and extend it to others. But if you can provide no reinforcement, the long-range prospects of adoption are slight; and if your recommendations will elicit punishing consequences for your listener, then you can predict with confidence that whatever his reactions may be at the time of the speech, he will eventually forget or reject what you offer him.

Assignment: Speech Preparation

During the preparation of your next speech for the classroom, answer the following questions:

1. What beliefs and values must your listeners share if they are to respond to this speech as you hope they will?
2. Are these beliefs and values conventional ones for all of your listeners? For a majority of them? For a sizeable minority of them?

3. What could go wrong with audience response if the audience does not in fact share these beliefs and values?

    a. If the majority of your auditors fails to share these attitudes and beliefs, what will be the effect on immediate response to the speech? Is the reaction of the majority likely to have an immediate effect on the remaining minority?

    b. For any given individual auditor, what will be the effect of his failure to share these attitudes and beliefs? How will this affect his long-range response?

Speech Experience Evaluation

Following your next classroom speech, be prepared to answer the following questions:

1. What was the activation level of the audience? Did it change during the speech? Did you do anything special to influence activation level?

2. Relative to your topic, what purposes might you have chosen other than the one you did choose? In retrospect, do you now believe that your choice of purpose was a wise one? How close did you come to accomplishing what you set out to do?

3. Were your assumptions about the knowledge and experience levels of your audience relative to your topic borne out by their observed reactions during the speech? Did you at any point bore them with details they already knew? Did you at any point lose them by assuming a higher level of knowledge and experience than they actually had?

chapter 6

ANALYSIS OF

AUDIENCE

AND OCCASION:

RELEVANCE

OF ROLES

Chapter 5 presented a rationale for audience analysis based on the importance of two sources of homogeneity in any natural audience, the tendency of people with similar traits to associate together, and the tendency of continued association to further increase the extent to which individuals share knowledge, attitudes, values, and beliefs. We have analyzed the influence that knowledge of the auditors has on the speaker's preparation and message content, and have explored the implications of some of the more important questions that serve as starting points for audience analysis.

This chapter will introduce the concept of *role* and will explore the significance of auditor roles in the over-all response of listeners—both in the immediate speech context and in terms of subsequent long-range behavior. Like the factors that served as the basis for our discussion in Chapter 5, role serves as a basis for homogeneity and predictability in audiences. The major purpose of the present chapter is to lay a foundation for understanding the concept and function of role, but some specific ways in which the role concept can be used to identify message effectiveness factors will also be discussed.

As a group member, an individual is cast in a particular *role*; that is, he occupies a position in the group such that he and his fellow members anticipate that he will behave predictably under certain circumstances. An analysis of audience role almost invariably leads the speaker to valuable information about his respondents' probable responses to his ideas, information, and appeals.

Consider for example Mr. J., a business executive. The role "Business Executive" is a meaningful one in our society, defined rather broadly by the set of circumstances, expectations, rewards, and punishments with which the individual finds himself confronted. The Business Executive, among other things, is punctual, hard-working, community-minded, alert to details, interested in people, and devoted to his company's advancement. Each of these traits suggests a wide range of specific values and behaviors which do in fact characterize business executives as distinguished, for example, from actors.

One reason why the role of Business Executive is defined by these terms is that the behaviors they symbolize lead to success in that role. Because of the way in which business organizations operate, men are usually rewarded for punctuality, alertness to detail, identification with company interest, etc., and are punished for the converse of these, and the rewards and punishments over a period of time condition the behavior of individuals filling the role. With the behavioral changes come changes in attitudes and perceptions which also contribute to success in the role. Because we tend to emulate success in others, the effects of reward and punishment are augmented by the effects of imitation when one executive discerns the sources of another's success.

PRESCRIPTION, DESCRIPTION, AND EXPECTATION

We shall get a broader view of role behavior if we consider Mr. K., a father. Like the role "Business Executive" the role "Father" is a meaningful one in our society, defined by the situation in which an individual filling that role finds himself. Though some subcultures may deviate markedly from the norm, in the majority of our society The Father is among other things moral, provident, and interested in children. At this point, however, we note some discrepancies between this role and the one mentioned earlier. While each of the father-traits mentioned above does suggest a wide range of specific values and behaviors, we are much less prepared to believe that these traits do in fact characterize fathers than we are to believe that the executive-traits characterize executives. We shall be in a better position to resolve the difficulty if we note that an individual role is defined in three different ways: prescription, description, and expectation.

Role *prescription* refers to those behaviors demanded of an individual occupying a particular role by the formal requirements of the group. The constitutions of most organizations, for example, provide that the president shall preside at meetings; the faculty handbook of a college may provide that professors shall maintain a stated number of office hours per week; a corporation manual of procedure may provide that the comptroller shall prepare a semi-annual financial report. Along another dimension, the doctrines of a religious group may prevent the consumption of certain foods or beverages or limit the forms of recreation in which a communicant may participate. Because such requirements and prohibitions are expressed formally, they are called prescriptive, and the sum total of all such requirements and prohibitions for a particular role is called the role prescription.

Role *description* refers to those behaviors that an individual occupying a particular role actually does perform. Generally, a role description includes most of the prescriptions for that same role, but often there are discrepancies. Students sometimes complain that professors, in spite of the faculty handbook, fail to maintain the required number of office hours. Moreover, there are on any campus certain behaviors that have become part of the professorial role but that have never been entered as formal prescriptions. At some colleges The Professor wears a tie and coat; at some he attends the student plays and symphonies; at some he entertains undergraduates in his home. Thus, many behaviors not included in the role prescription appear in the role description, that is, in the sum total of those things which an individual actually does within a particular role.

Role *expectation* refers to those behaviors which an individual occupying a given role is expected by other members of the group to perform. Of all aspects of role, this is the most complex, for expectations are a function of some reference group and very few roles have their significance within a single group only. For example, certain things are expected of The Executive by other members of his business organization. If the organization is large, the expectations of his subordinates, of his superiors, and of his office staff may vary somewhat. Moreover, his fellow-executives in other companies will also have certain expectations concerning the behavior of The Executive, which may differ somewhat from the expectations of the various groups in his own corporation. The point is that role expectations are relative to some particular group, and if the same role is significant to more than one group then the expectations for that role may differ from one of the concerned groups to another. This is not at all surprising, since role expectation is at least partly the result of group needs, and these may be expected to differ from one group to another.

What is a little surprising is that the expectations of various groups concerning the same role seldom conflict. Sometimes the differing expectations are mutually reinforcing: Mr. J's secretary expects to be rewarded for her efforts; Mr. J's boss expects him to maintain a satisfied office staff; both expectations are satisfied if Mr. J. gives the secretary a raise. Even when differing expectations are not mutually reinforcing they are often compatible: Mr. K's son expects Father's companionship; his wife expects Father to keep the car clean; if Mr. K. enlists his son's help in washing the car, and they chat while doing so, then both expectations can be satisfied. Frustrating conflicts may arise when two reference groups carry differing and incompatible expectations concerning the same role; but such conflicts are comparatively rare.

Moreover, one finds in general a high degree of compatibility between role prescription, role description, and role expectation. In those cases where large-scale incompatibilities exist among these three entities group morale tends to be lowered and group efficiency impaired. Moreover, the individual in a role where prescriptions, descriptions, and expectations are at odds with one another finds himself in a potentially uncomfortable situation.

ROLE CONFORMITY

We are now in a better position to discuss The Father role, in which we noted some ambiguity earlier. That a father shall provide for his children is a role *prescription* established by law. That he be moral and interested in children is not a matter of prescription, but it is a role *expectation* for the majority of society. Within the confines of the home, of course, expectations (perhaps based on experience) may differ from society's concerning the behaviors of The Father. In this case, the father in question will be aware of the differing expectations of these two reference groups and may behave differently in one situation than in the other. Even most fathers who are immoral and/or disinterested in children will feign these fatherly "virtues" if they can, in order to avoid the unpleasant social consequences of behaving otherwise publicly. Thus when we say that The Father is provident, moral, and interested in children we refer to the public social role expectation—one to which most fathers will make some effort to respond. This is merely a special case of the more general rule that individuals will in general seek to fulfill what they recognize as the role expectations of their reference groups in all of their relations with those groups.

Several features of this principle of role conformity require special emphasis. First, one can respond only to those role prescriptions and expectations of which he is aware at the time.

Unknown or unrecognized expectations cannot influence behavior.

Second, role will have its most profound effect upon that behavior which the individual perceives to be related to the group in which the role is held. For instance, a Methodist behaves most characteristically like The Methodist in church or in the presence of other Methodists. The difference of his behavior in other contexts does not, as is generally believed, necessarily grow out of insincerity or hypocrisy, but is a reflection of differences in context. In the church context the behaviors of others invoke and support in him The Methodist role; but in other contexts the supporting stimuli for the role behaviors are absent. Later on, when we talk more about reference groups, we shall see that this statement needs some qualification, but for the moment it is important to realize that role behavior tends to be most characteristic when the individual is in the group within which the role is defined, or when he believes that his behavior will be of consequence to that group. When we state that a person is "rigid" or "inflexible" in his behavior, we may be saying that he insists on maintaining the role behavior of a particular group while he is associating with other groups.

A third point is closely related to the second. An individual can be predicted to engage in behavior characteristic of a role only when the role has been invoked. Few people occupy a single role all or even most of the time; most people have a fairly sizeable number of different roles which alternate depending upon the circumstances in which the individual finds himself. When a given set of circumstances comes to elicit a characteristic pattern of behaviors for an individual, then for that individual those circumstances may be said to invoke the role described by those behaviors. By "circumstances" we mean any combination of stimuli, simple or complex. Thus a church full of people represents one circumstance sufficient to induce in some people The Methodist role. On the other hand, the same role may be invoked in other people by such simple stimuli as the occurrence of an idea theme—such as "The Preflectability of Mankind" in a speech or an essay.

A final point is that, once invoked, a role may exert a powerful influence over the individual occupying it, so that he behaves in accordance with the role even though he would otherwise prefer not to do so. Many extremely powerful strategies of persuasion rely upon the invocation of dominant roles. To return to The Father, the male parent generally finds it most difficult to resist strong sales appeals for life insurance unless he is already oversubscribed, simply because the image of Father as Provider is such a central aspect of The Father role in our culture. Few fathers can withstand for long arguments based on the premise that they are not doing everything possible to provide for their families. Under the influence of this role expectation The Father can be induced to buy insurance that he really does not want on any other ground than "living up to" the role in which he has been cast.

To prove that the persuasive power of the life-insurance salesman's appeal rests indeed upon role, one has only to notice that the very same arguments are almost universally ineffective with The Mother, whose role includes little expectation of providence if The Father is still living.[1]

The preceding section is not intended to deprecate either the motives or the methods of life-insurance salesmen. Indeed, the insurance salesman in this context could be viewed as an instrument of society calling deviant fathers to the more perfect performance of their roles. But whether we view the salesman as opportunist or social therapist, the interaction between salesman and client underscores the point that roles sometimes control behavior to an inordinate degree, sometimes even contrary to the private wishes of the role occupant.

---

[1]Under the multiple social and economic pressures of contemporary American culture, the role of The Father is changing. In particular, the providence function is coming to be shared more nearly equally by both parents. As a consequence we should find women buying more life insurance.

REFERENCE GROUPS

It is essential for the speaker to remember that role behavior is supported by social groups. The group that reinforces a particular role is called the reference group for that role. To a considerable extent the dominance of any role in a given individual is closely related to the importance he attaches to his membership in that role's reference group.[2]

Individuals occupying a given role may vary a great deal with respect to how important that role is to them. Mr. W., The Weekend Pilot, may find that role much more important to him than it is to Mr. N., The Weekend Pilot. This is particularly likely if Mr. W. belongs to a flying club or has regular contacts with other Weekend Pilots. We could predict that, other things being equal, Mr. W. would be more interested in communication about flying than Mr. N., would have more information about it, and would be open to a wider range of persuasive appeals based on it than would Mr. N.

It is characteristic of individuals to whom membership in a given group is quite important that they tend to gravitate toward positions of leadership in that group. Thus the PTA member who is most interested in the organization, knows most about it, and is most open to appeals emanating from it is quite likely to eventually become the PTA President. Whether involvement produces leadership or leadership produces involvement is an intriguing—but probably pointless—question; the essential point is that leadership and involvement do tend very strongly to go hand in hand. On this basis we should expect Mr.

[2]It is in fact possible to discuss all of the concepts we have here discussed under "role" entirely in terms of the individual's relationships with various reference groups. We have chosen to discuss these issues in terms of roles because we believe that this representation is both simpler and in closer agreement with everyday experience. But it is essential to remember that every aspect of role behavior is intimately related to reference groups.

W. to move toward a position of greater leadership in flying groups than Mr. N., increasing still further the range of his behavior dominated by his role in these groups. To the speaker it is important to bear in mind that the leaders in any group are most inclined to respond to appeals based on the norms and concepts of that group.

Although many roles are susceptible to such differential treatment by different individuals, some roles are so defined by their reference groups that they cover an extremely large segment of the behavior of any individual who occupies them, whatever his interests might otherwise be. Two such roles are The Physician and The Military Officer.

It is characteristic of very powerful groups that they define roles which are preemptive and which cover an extremely wide range of behavior. Virtually all religious groups seek to extend such broad and preemptive control over the behaviors of their communicants, as do political conspiracies such as The Communist Party. Such groups call for—and often get—"absolute loyalty and obedience"; that is, the member tries to play the role all of the time, and always behaves as though he were under the direct scrutiny of other members of the group.

Persons whose identification with a particular reference group is so strong that they always play the role assigned to them by that group present a curious problem in persuasion. Recommendations coming with reference group approval and growing out of reference group concepts tend to be utterly persuasive; few other appeals carry much weight. Moreover, when such an individual is present in a mixed audience, he will tend to perceive himself as a "representative" of his reference group and so behave in a fashion foreign to that of others who are relatively freer to adopt roles more appropriate. When, for example, a Communist heckles the speaker at a non-Communist political rally he is merely responding to the situation as every good Communist by definition should. He is playing his role as it was defined for him; and it matters little that the behaviors of the other audience members do not support his own, for the immediate audience is not the reference group to which the behavior is directed. The boos and catcalls are really intended for the ears of his fellow-conspirators; and if the cell in which he received his training has done its job well, he will find his antisocial behavior gratifying in itself whether there are other Communists present to hear him or not. When this condition has been reached, the behavior has become autonomous, and in a sense the individual may be said to have internalized the reference group. To such an individual the physical presence of the reference group is not necessary to support the role behaviors.

Because a role is defined and supported by a social system, it tends to be more or less independent of the individuals who fill it; and because the role exerts upon the individual pressures to conform to the behaviors appropriate to the role, an individual's behavior becomes much more predictable when he acts with a socially defined role. As we have noted, this increase in predictability extends to the individual's responses to communication, making the analysis of auditor roles a productive approach to audience analysis.

RECOGNIZING THE AUDITOR'S ROLE

We have already seen some of the uses to which role analysis can be put. Another important implication of audience roles is that communication addressed to the listener *in the role which he is playing* in the speech situation will be more acceptable (appropriate), clearer, more interesting, and more persuasive than communication addressed to some other role, even if it is one that he often plays. Humor is unacceptable in most ceremonial addresses because who the listeners are and what they think themselves to be doing on such occasions—that is, their roles—do not allow them to respond in any appropriate fashion to humor, even that which they would enjoy immensely in some other role; laughing is not a ceremonial behavior.

The foregoing example demonstrates that behavior inconsistent with the listener's momentary role is often perceived as inappropriate. Furthermore, it may also be confusing. Unless the topic is very carefully introduced, a speech describing the United Fund community services is not likely to receive much attention at a Country Club dinner dance, because the topic is out of character with the role the listeners are playing at the moment. Due to this inattention caused by incompatibility between message and receiver-role, the listener to such a speech is likely to find the speaker's message unclear. With special effort, of course, the speaker may increase the likelihood of a favorable response, but he will find it easiest to do so if he understands that the listener's present momentary role is a barrier to clear understanding.

Role-consistent communication is not only more appropriate and clearer, but it is more interesting as well. At the PTA meeting, Mr. L. will listen with real interest to an informative talk by the school superintendent on the elementary school guidance program, even though he might find this topic of relatively little interest in any other context. In the PTA member role he may have some very specialized interests which he displays to a much lesser extent in other circumstances. Such considerations, of course, do not extend to an individual's intense or life-long interests; but for most of us the number of such interests is relatively small, and most of the things we are interested in are associated in some way with the various roles we play. These interests tend to wax and wane as we shift from one role to another.

In addition to its appropriateness, clarity, and interest, role-consistent communication is also more persuasive. It should be much easier to persuade an individual to contribute a sum of money to his Alma Mater in his role as Mr. O., The Old Grad, than in most of the other roles he plays. This stems from the expectations surrounding the role, which provide very convenient sources of persuasive appeals. Thus any set of circumstances that will invoke and support the role will tend to make The Old Grad more susceptible to persuasive appeals for donations than he otherwise would be.

Earlier we noted that audiences are not random or accidental collections of individuals, but that each member of an audience is there for a specific reason. Usually that reason grows out of his commitment to some group, and it follows that the role he plays in that group will affect his interpretation of and response to what the speaker has to say. It may therefore be profitable for the speaker to inquire what brings his auditors to the speech, what roles they will play as they hear it, and what reference groups will shape their responses to it. In some cases this inquiry may be extremely difficult and the answers hard to obtain; ordinarily, however, very useful answers will lie close at hand.

SOCIAL FACILITATION

In the previous chapter we stated that there were notable exceptions to the rule that it is easier to achieve a given object in conversation with a single individual than through public speaking to a group. We now are in a position to recognize those exceptions. They occur when the nature of the audience and occasion are such that it is possible to invoke and sustain a role that it might be very difficult to invoke and maintain on a one-to-one basis. If the response sought is one that may occur in such a socially facilitated role and is extremely unlikely to occur otherwise, and if the role is one which the speaker is able to invoke in the situation in which he finds his audience, then it will be easier to achieve his purpose with his listeners as a group than with those same listeners one at a time.

ROLE CONFLICT

We have already noted that an individual ordinarily possesses a number of different roles, at least one for every group to which he belongs. Mr. J., The Business Executive, and Mr. K., The Father, often meet in a single individual, who may also be Mr. L., The PTA Member, Mr. M., The Methodist, Mr. N., The Weekend Pilot, and Mr. O., The Old Grad. We have also suggested that this multiplicity of roles ordinarily causes no problems because the circumstances that invoke any one of the roles ordinarily do not invoke any of the others: one situation—one role is the principle which generally operates.

Striking exceptions to this general principle do occur, however, and the communicator planning to use speech as an instrument of social action should understand what may happen when they do.

Sometimes a single set of circumstances invokes two roles simultaneously; that is, the individual is aware of "having a responsibility" to two reference groups at the same time. When the individual perceives that the role expectations of the two groups support the same behavior, that behavior is facilitated. If on the other hand the roles conflict, then a state of tension exists until the conflict can be resolved.

The multiple-role problem is significant for the public speaker because he may choose to function as an invoker of roles, and in doing so needs to understand some of the consequences of role facilitation and role conflict.

First of all, the speaker needs to understand that in most public-speaking situations the audience members are present in well-defined roles, and that the speaker's ability to invoke other roles is to some extent limited by this fact. The stronger and better supported are the audience roles created by the speaking situation, the more difficult will it be to invoke any other roles at all. Moreover, even where some opportunity is available, it is usually quite difficult for a public speaker to invoke roles incompatible with that in which the audience is cast at the moment. One reason for this is that the auditor will typically have cast the speaker himself in a role complementary to his own, and in that role will have expectations of him. If the speaker departs too dramatically from these expectations he may be rejected without a hearing.

Usually the speaker will find opportunities in the auditors' momentary role to develop their interest, understanding, and acceptance of his point of view. When he invokes other roles, he will usually find it most useful to invoke those which facilitate similar behaviors. Certainly the speaker can take advantage of the fact that behavior supported by multiple roles is more gratifying than behavior supported by only one.

The rule in the case of role facilitation is quite simple: that behavior is most likely which is supported by the greatest number of role expectations. However, when two roles suggest conflicting behaviors some decision principle must be employed to resolve the difficulty. In fact, three principles appear to be involved, which for the sake of convenience we may call role valuation, immediate context, and primary behavioral reference.

The principle of *role valuation* implies that every individual attaches different values to each of the roles in which he is cast, so that these may be arranged in a hierarchy from most- to least-valued. The principle states that *in cases of role conflict, other things being equal, that behavior will be selected which is supported by the most valued role.*

The principle of *immediate context* implies that a given context provides greater support for some roles than for others. The Sunday morning worship service provides more support for The Methodist role than for The Business Executive role. The principle states that *in cases of role conflict, other things being equal, that behavior will be selected which is most strongly supported by the immediate context.*

The principle of *primary behavioral reference* implies that a behavior that is relevant to two or more roles will be perceived as more deeply involved in some roles than in others. Roles to which a behavior is understood to be highly relevant serve as primary references for that behavior. The principle states that *in cases of role conflict, other things being equal, that role will dominate behavior which serves as a primary reference for the behavior.*

Thus, before inducing role conflict in his audience the speaker may wish to consider how these three principles will operate to resolve the conflict he induces. If the behavior desired by the speaker is supported by a role that his listeners value very highly, then he may feel rather safe inducing the role conflict, provided the competing behavior is not related to a role having a great deal of support in the immediate context of the speech and providing the conflicting role does not serve as a primary reference for the undesired behavior.

On the other hand, the speaker must take account of the fact that role conflicts are painful and, whatever the outcome, almost always leave traces of dissatisfaction. If the desired attitude or behavior must be sustained over a period of time following the communication, this dissatisfaction may lead the listener to seek alternate courses of action or—what is more likely—try to avoid the behavioral choice altogether.

INFLUENCE OF ROLE
ON LONG-TERM COMMUNICATION EFFECTS

A final point that must be kept in mind is that, although a speech is a brief and transitory event, roles persist over long periods of time. Any communication that enables an individual to function more satisfactorily in any of his roles will be constantly reinforced by the social system and so will continue to influence the individual's behavior over a considerable period. Moreover, if the communication leads to adaptive behavioral changes, then other occupants of similar roles, observing the successful behavior in this listener, will emulate it, so that the effects of the speech will spread.

If, on the other hand, the effect of the communication is maladaptive, if it causes the individual to function in a less satisfactory way in any of his roles, then the communication will not be reinforced and its influence, however great it might have been at the time of utterance, will soon dissipate.

After a speech is over life goes on. The long-term effect of the speech is a direct function of the extent to which it integrates with the listener's ongoing experience and in some sense improves it. Surely the speaker will find ways to be more effective if he is able to discover what the quality of his listener's experience is. It has been the purpose of this chapter to suggest some guides for doing so.

Assignment: Speech Preparation

In preparing your next speech to the class, consider the relation of the content of your proposed speech to the audience:

1. What roles do you anticipate your material will evoke in the context of the classroom speaking situation?
2. What reference group(s) will come into play for your listeners as you proceed?
3. What will the material you are presenting do to enhance or inhibit your listeners' effectiveness in any of the roles they will play following the speech?

Self-Analysis of Response to Communication

During the next round of speeches in class, choose one speech in advance and plan to make a detailed self-analysis of your response to that speech. Note during the speech what roles are evoked as the speech unfolds (that is, what roles are evoked for *you*—other roles might be evoked for other listeners).

Note what aspects of the situation, the speech, or the speaker produced these effects. Did it appear that it was the speaker's intent to evoke these roles? Where they conducive to his purpose, or did they inhibit the response he sought?

Note what reference group(s) you used in listening to the

speech. Did it appear that the speaker anticipated these reference groups correctly? Did they enhance or inhibit the response that the speaker seemed to be seeking?

chapter 7

DELIVERY

As an instrument of social action, a public speech is something more than the documentary record of its text. So far, most of the details of its planning have had to do with the relation of its content to the characteristics and roles of its auditors and with the relation of the speaker's purposes to the broad social fabric in which the contemplated social action is proposed; but, however far-reaching its implications may be, it produces its effects through some immediate audience, and it elicits responses from them only as it is presented to them in visible and audible form. A speech must be spoken to have any effect.

How important is the manner of speaking in determining the outcome of the speech event? In what ways can we describe and evaluate the details of the speaker's manner? Around these questions have grown up a considerable folklore and a fair-sized body of reliable research findings. In this chapter we shall explore ways of describing the speech act and, where possible, suggest standards of evaluation based on the findings of research. We shall be less concerned with how to deliver a speech than with what the elements of delivery are and how we can reason about standards of excellence and effectiveness.

INTRODUCTION

The act of speaking, which is so natural and easy for most people, is in fact the most highly patterned and complex behavior universally practiced in human societies. To speaker and auditor alike the speech act is simple and unitary; under ordinary conditions neither perceives it as a complicated sequence of events or as an intricate constellation of elements. Nevertheless, the study of speech behavior and its effects has led to the discovery of a growing number of variables and increasingly more complex relations among them.

This chapter will focus on those variables having to do with the audible and visible properties of the speech act that are usually discussed under the heading of "delivery." In restricting our attention to these matters, it will be necessary to hold two qualifications clearly in mind.

First, any effort to discuss these variables in isolation must result in certain distortions, for though we may talk about them independently they in fact never exist alone. "Delivery" is not an object or an event, but is instead an *aspect* of the speech act. It never occurs outside the context created by a speaker addressing an auditor on some occasion in certain language concerning a particular idea. Because the variety of such contexts is infinite, and because context influences the manner in which the delivery variables are received and take effect, any general discussion of delivery will overemphasize the significance of a given variable for one context while underemphasizing it for another. In reading this chapter it is important to remember that it is the specific speech context rather than any general set of requirements that dictates which delivery variables are important on a given occasion.

Second, as we examine some of these variables and relationships, it is important to bear in mind that for the most part they exist and have their effect outside the awareness of both speaker and listener. The attention of the participants in any communication transaction will ordinarily be drawn to other matters, and only rarely will delivery variables serve as objects of their direct attention. These variables are important because they enable the observer of such transactions to describe and understand them more completely. It is therefore important to remember that the details we shall note are introduced from the standpoint of the outside "objective" observer, whose task it is to describe the act of speaking and to trace its effects, rather than from the viewpoint of the speaker or listener, who see the speech from entirely different "subjective" points of view.

We will discuss first certain features of the apparatus by means of which the speaker emits patterns of behavior capable of serving as stimuli for his auditors. Second, we will discuss certain variables of delivery as they exist in the sound and sight channels between speaker and listener. Finally, we will discuss some relationships between these variables and certain features of audience response.

THE MECHANICS OF TRANSMISSION

In at least one important respect, the manner in which a speaker transmits a speech to an audience is similar to the way in which a television station transmits a broadcast to a receiving set. In neither case does there exist a fixed physical connection between the source and the receiver: the source must employ a transmitting apparatus to generate physical energies which can pass through some channel in a form that serves as stimuli for the receiver. In face-to-face speaking, communication ordinarily takes place through visual and auditory channels. The speaker's behavior generates patterns of visual and acoustic energy, which are capable of stimulating the auditor's eye and ear, somewhat in the way that broadcast signals energize systems in the television set when the power is turned on and the set adjusted to the available signal frequency.

VOICE PRODUCTION.

The acoustic energies of speech are produced by the vocal tract, which consists of specific structures of the chest, neck, and head. The process by which speech sounds are produced may be divided into four stages: respiration, phonation, resonation, and articulation.

The production of speech begins with *respiration,* in the first stage of which the diaphragm and intercostal muscles contract so as to increase the capacity of the chest, creating a partial vacuum which causes air to pass from outside the body through the mouth or nose, down the trachea and bronchi, and into the lungs. The controlled expulsion of this column of air enclosed in the lungs and trachea provides the basic energy for the second phase of voice production.

Located at the top of the trachea and opening into the base of the throat is a boxlike structure of bone and cartilage called the larynx, which contains a pair of liplike structures called the vocal folds. In normal respiration these are held in an open, relaxed position, allowing free passage of air. However, in voice production the vocal folds are approximated so that air must force its way between them in order to escape the lungs. When this occurs, the escaping air causes the vocal folds to vibrate rapidly releasing air in tiny puffs at the rate of 100 to 200 times per second. These tiny puffs set into vibration the entire column of air in the vocal tract, providing the basic vocal tone. The action by which they are produced is called *phonation,* the second phase of voice production.

The complex tone produced by phonation is a weak and relatively unharmonious sound. It is modified into a strong and recognizably human voice by the process of *resonation.* The laryngeal tone contains many harmonics; that is, it contains sound energy at a great many frequencies, so that a single laryngeal tone is composed of a great number of sounds ranging from high to low, all occurring simultaneously. The cavities of the throat, mouth, and nasal passages, acting as resonators, amplify certain of the laryngeal frequencies making them sound louder than the rest. The resulting vocal tone is both louder and more harmonious than the unresonated laryngeal tone. By changing the size and shape of the mouth and throat, and raising or lowering the velum (the trailing edge of the soft palate) to allow less or more resonance in the nasal cavities, it is possible to produce

many strikingly different vocal sounds from the same basic laryngeal tone.

The lips, teeth, tongue, and palate work together to shape,
restrict, or interrupt the resonated vocal tone in such a way as
to produce the recognizable sounds of speech in a process called
articulation. The use of different forms of articulation makes
possible a great variety of distinctly different speech sounds, the
vowels and consonants. Sequences of such distinctive sounds are
strung together in rapid succession like beads on a chain, to
form words, which are the basic units of meaningful discourse.

MUSCULAR ACTIVITY.

Man does not speak with words alone, for simultaneously with
the production of acoustic energies in the vocal tract, the
muscles of the speaker's whole body are engaged in behavior
which produces patterns of visual stimuli for the listener. A
point that is often overlooked is that the speaker is not free to
choose whether or not to emit visible behavior; for even if he
stands perfectly still without moving a muscle he is nevertheless
engaged in bodily activity—in this case a most extraordinary
pattern of activity—which will be quite visible to all of his auditors. The speaker may, of course, choose not to control his patterns of bodily activity; but in this case the visible behavior is
not missing, it is merely operating outside the speaker's conscious control.

Whereas the acoustic energies of speech are created almost
exclusively by the vocal tract, visible behavior is emitted by as
much of the speaker's body as the auditor can see. It follows that
every skeletal muscle is a potential transmitter of visual messages. However, due to their fine musculature, great flexibility,
and high visibility under most conditions, the face and hands
appear to command a greater share of the listener's attention
than other parts of the body, and are more often subjected to
the speaker's deliberate control.

THE VARIABLES OF DELIVERY

The actions of the speaker's vocal tract and external musculature produce patterns of energy in the sight and sound channels between him and his auditor. These patterns are, of course, quite complex and are susceptible to analysis from a number of different points of view. The phonetician is interested in the acoustic properties of the individual sounds, the linguist in the temporal sequence of sounds, the kinesicist in the information carried by the code of visible action, the voice scientist in the sound spectrum of the voice, and the elocutionist in the relationship of certain patterns of visible and audible behavior to the verbal content of the speech. From the standpoint of effectiveness in public speaking, it has proved useful to pay special attention to certain characteristics of the speaker's visible and audible behavior. These characteristics are the variables of delivery, which may be divided for purposes of preliminary analysis into those that exist in the auditory channel and have to do with voice, and those that exist in the visual channel and have to do with bodily action. In each case, a set of primary and a set of secondary variables may be discerned.

Voice

PRIMARY VARIABLES.

The primary vocal variables are those that characterize our reception of any complex tone: pitch, loudness, quality, and duration. Other properties that we hear in the voice result from various combinations of these four.

Pitch refers to the location of a tone on the musical scale, and corresponds to the fundamental frequency of the sound waves striking the ear. The fundamental frequency of the voice is the frequency of its lowest component—in the case of the average male speaker around 80 to 120 cycles per second. In a voice of good quality, most of the other components to the vocal tone are harmonics of this fundamental frequency (that is, whole multiples of it). In general the pitch of male voices is considerably lower than that of female voices. All normal voices are capable of producing a wide range of different pitch levels, and customarily do so in natural speaking. Expecially in animated conversation the voice seldom remains at a single pitch level for more than a fraction of a second, but moves rapidly up and down the scale. The highest-pitched and lowest-pitched tones that a speaker can produce comfortably will define his pitch range. Ordinarily his average pitch falls about one-third of the way up from the bottom of his pitch range.

Loudness corresponds to the amplitude of the sound waves striking the ear. Just as the normal voice is constantly changing in pitch, so too is it constantly shifting in loudness. Speakers differ as much in customary average loudness as they do in average pitch. In some societies there is a tendency for women to speak more softly than men, but this does not appear to be generally so in the United States and Europe.

Quality refers to the subtle blending of harmonics, which is partly responsible for our ability to distinguish one voice from another. The terminology in which voice qualities are described is highly subjective, making any systematic discussion of the topic extremely difficult. Most people are able to recognize such deviant qualities as nasality, harshness, breathiness, and hoarseness, but beyond this list even voice specialists differ concerning the proper designation of voice qualities. This disagreement is particularly true regarding the qualities that are considered admirable. Voices have been described as orotund, mellifluous, twanging, syrupy, metallic, grating, honeyed, warm, resonant, penetrating, and husky. The quality of any given speaker's voice tends to remain relatively constant under most conditions, and to be as distinctive as a fingerprint; but voice quality tends to change under the influence of emotion and it is possible for most speakers to alter it voluntarily to some extent.

Duration refers to the temporal extensiveness of sounds and silences in speech. As we indicated in the preceding section, an utterance consists of a series of vowels and consonants following one another in rapid succession. The average duration of each of these individual sounds in ordinary speaking is just under 1/5 second, with the vowels for the most part requiring considerably more and the consonants considerably less time. The vowels especially are highly flexible in duration, and tend to lengthen or shorten according to the mood of the speaker.[1] Among other well-known speakers of the day, U.S. Senator Everett Dirksen, former President John F. Kennedy, and Cuban Premier Fidel Castro achieved certain oratorical effects by manipulating vowel length, though each has done so in a different way.

The stream of speech is not continuous, but is interrupted by innumerable silences of varying duration. The ear is capable of detecting very short silences, and we are accustomed to attach special significance to silences of 1/10 second or longer. If such a silence occurs at the end of a phrase, or before an emphasized word, or in some other meaningful context, it is called a pause; otherwise it is a hesitation or nonfluency. Pauses vary from 1/10 second to several seconds in duration, with shorter pauses occurring vastly more often than longer ones. It is likely that frequency and average duration of pauses increases with audience size and with the formality of the occasion, though pauses of greater than three seconds are rare even for large audiences and very formal situations.[2]

[1] Grant Fairbanks and LeMar W. Hoaglin, "An Experimental Study of the Durational Characteristics of the Voice During the Expression of Emotion," *Speech Monographs*, VIII (1941), 85–90.

[2] Jack A. Samosky, "A Study of John F. Kennedy's Rate of Speaking under Three Conditions," unpublished MA Thesis, University of Wisconsin, 1961.

SECONDARY VARIABLES.

In addition to the primary vocal variables of pitch, loudness, quality, and duration, which are concerned with the elementary properties of the voice, certain secondary variables, derived from the primary ones by combining with each other and with certain linguistic variables, are known to influence the effectiveness of speech. These secondary vocal variables are inflection, stress, fluency, and dialect.

Inflection is concerned with changes in pitch over very short intervals of time. We just noted that in natural speech the pitch of the voice never remains constant for more than a fraction of a second, but is constantly moving up and down the scale in a series of steps and glides. An inflectional step occurs when a word or syllable ends at one pitch and the succeeding word or syllable begins at another. A clear example of a downward step occurs in the common expression "oh-oh," as it ocurs in situations of surprise or discovery. The first "oh" occurs at a relatively high pitch, then there is a sudden break, and the second "oh" is uttered at a considerably lower pitch. In animated conversation many steps both downward and upward occur.

Smooth changes of pitch during the utterance of a vowel are called glides. An upward glide is used by most American speakers on the last syllable of a question and in the traditional way of answering the telephone, where the last vowel of the word "hello" is uttered on a prolonged rising inflection. On the other hand, most factual statements end on a falling glide. Inflections tend to characterize the mood of the speaker, so that the manner of inflection is taken by most listeners as a partial indication of the speaker's emotional state and attitude toward his listener and/or topic of conversation. The way in which inflections transmit impressions of the speaker's emotions to the listener is by no means clearly understood, but a simple experiment will show the extent of their effect. Each of the three greetings printed below will suggest a different shade of warmth and friendliness, as well as a different relationship that the speaker feels between himself and his auditor.

Stress refers to changes of loudness in time, the stressed syllables or words being those which are uttered with greater loudness. Correct pronunciation of polysyllabic English words requires three degrees of stress, which most children have mastered by school age. In the word "re-establish," for example, the third syllable receives primary stress, the first syllable receives secondary stress, and the second and fourth syllables are unstressed. However, when words are combined in a context, special stress is often employed to call attention to a particular word or syllable. For instance, if the word "re-establish" were used in a context which also included the word "establish," ordinary usage would dictate primary emphasis on the first syllable, in order to bring out the contrast between the two words and reduce the likelihood of misunderstanding.

Fluency refers to the smoothness and rapidity of speech, and seems closely related to the perceived ease and naturalness of the speaker. If the rate of speech is quite slow, or if there are many hesitations, or if the speaker tends to repeat words or to leave sentences incomplete, then the speech is perceived as nonfluent. In an extemporaneous utterance few speakers are able to avoid nonfluencies altogether for more than two or three sentences at a time. As a matter of fact, one of the chief distinctions between extemporaneous speech on the one hand and rehearsed speech and oral reading on the other is the great difference in fluency ordinarily observed.

Dialect is a complex variable, which may involve any or all of the variables discussed so far. Although the term "dialect" is used commonly to refer to "different" or "substandard" speech, a stricter interpretation of term leads to the realization that everybody speaks one dialect or another. Thus, in some portions of the United States, the word "house" is pronounced HAUS, in others it is pronounced HAHS, and in still others it is pronounced HEHWS. Which of these pronunciations is "normal" and which is "dialectal" varies according to the geographical location of the speaker and listener. That is, the difference between a "quaint dialect" and "standard speech" exists in the listener, not in the speech pattern.

In addition to differnces in pronunciation, dialect may involve inflectional, durational, and quality differences as well. Thus, though it is typical of most American dialects to end a question with a rising inflection as we indicated above, in certain sections of the East a question is not "asked" but "told"— that is, the question sentence ends on falling inflection. Differences in duration may be dialect as well. A "drawl" is accomplished partly by extending the duration of certain vowels. As for quality, parts of the Southwest are characterized in part by the vocal qualities of harshness and nasality, described acoustically as the presence of inharmonic frequencies and a concentration of resonance in the upper-middle pitch range coupled with damping or the elimination of overtones from a lower pitch range. In its broadest sense, dialect refers to any difference in utterance that distinguishes the people of one geographical region or social class from those of another region or class, and the number of possible differences is extremely large.

Bodily Action

PRIMARY VARIABLES.

The primary variables of bodily action are those that characterize our visual perception of any muscular activity. They are: tone, position, and action.

A muscle consists of a very large number of small fibers, each of which is capable of contracting more or less independently of the others. In no healthy muscle are all of these fibers relaxed at the same time, which is to say that every healthy muscle is always contracted to some degree. The degree of contraction (that is, the number of individual fibers that are contracted), varying over a wide range from extremely mild contraction during sleep to very pronounced during violent exertion, is called tonus or muscle tone. Muscles display greater tone when one is alert than when he is not, and still greater tone when he is tense than when he is merely alert. Within broad limits, the degree of muscle tone is a visible characteristic of the organism, and thus capable of carrying information concerning the extent to which it is energized, motivated, or involved.

Position is a relative term, and when used with respect to bodily action refers to the static positions of the various parts of the body with respect to each other. Certain fixed positions of the body and of particular parts of it are especially noticeable and so may be invested with special significance: the open palm, extended index finger, raised arm, forward inclination of the body, and smile are examples of static positions that may take on particular significance in a given situation.

Action refers to movement from one position to another. It is characterized by frequency, extensiveness, and rate. Frequency refers to the number of distinguishable movements, extensiveness refers to the size or magnitude of an individual movement, and rate refers to the speed with which the individual movement is performed. A speaker's action may be frequent or rare, large or small, fast or slow. Frequent, small, rapid movements obviously present a vastly different visual picture than infrequent, large, slow ones.

SECONDARY VARIABLES.

The combination of tone, position, and action for certain areas of the body has received special treatment from students of speech. These combinations are the secondary variables of bodily action: facial expression, posture, gesture, and movement.

Facial expression refers to the tone, position, and action of the facial muscles. Facial expressions typically are described as static positions, representable by a sketch or still photograph. Unquestionably the fixed positions do contain a good deal of information about the presumed emotional or attitudinal condition of the speaker; but evidence indicates that action adds a good deal more information. The combination of action and position, representable by a silent motion picture of the face, apparently leads viewers to rather consistent impressions concerning the attitudes of the speaker, even when they are unable to hear his words. Of course, these consistent impressions may be entirely wrong and sometimes are; but, the important point here is that viewers are fairly consistent concerning what they *think* they see in the positions and actions of the speaker's face.[3]

Posture refers to the position and tone of the large parts of the speaker's body relative to one another: the head, trunk, arms, and legs. The speaker who leans forward slightly toward the audience is displaying a postural difference from the speaker who rests back on his heels, leaning slightly away from the audience. This latter posture is accentuated when accompanied by arms folded across the chest. The slight difference in total bodily orientation is apparently interpreted by many listeners as a reflection of the speaker's attitude and intentions, as is a limp, flaccid over-all tone.

Gesture refers to actions of particular parts of the body, particularly of the hand, arm, shoulder, and head. While it is proper to call any such action a gesture, the term is most commonly applied to specific action patterns which are repeated, either by a speaker or in a particular society, often enough to become noticeable or perhaps even to assume a generally fixed significance. Especially in the latter case the gesture will usually be characterized by a fixed position, such as the extended arm,

---

[3]L. Carmichael, S. O. Roberts, and N. Y. Wessell, "A Study of the Judgment of Manual Expression as Presented in Still and Motion Pictures," *Journal of Social Psychology*, VIII (1937), 115–43.

though the gesture as a whole consists of the movement toward that position and the withdrawal away from it, as well as the position itself.

Movement consists of the action of the legs and torso, and should not be confused with gesture. A speaker may gesture much and move little, or gesture little and move much. The speaker who paces back and forth, who alternately leans toward the audience and away from it, or who sways from side to side is engaged in movement.

EFFECTS OF DELIVERY

Though most writers on public speaking are wary of the subject, and many students are inclined to suspect its value, every serious analysis of public speaking has eventually been required to consider the topic of delivery, for there are certain effects that regularly occur in audiences which cannot be explained in any other way. Thus the topic of delivery is an important consideration in public speaking, both in its own right and in connection with other variables in the speech and in the audience. Let us look at the ways in which delivery contributes to some of the effects of a speech.

Information Gain

One type of communication effect may be said to occur when the listener understands something that the speaker has said. Such an effect can be inferred when the listener can repeat points or statements made by the speaker, or when he can answer correctly a question about the information content of the speech. Delivery variables play a significant but highly complex role in the production of effects of this type.

To begin with, the speaker's voice must reach the listener's ear with sufficient intensity to serve as a carrier of information; if the voice cannot be heard and the speech sounds distinguished, it is clear that no information will be conveyed. However, this does not imply that loudness is an important consideration for every speaker under all circumstances. Most people speak loudly and clearly enough to achieve a satisfactory standard of intelligibility under ordinary conditions, including most public-speaking situations.

On the other hand, there are certain extraordinary conditions under which the loudness of the voice can become a decisive consideration in the transmission of information. One of these is the special case of the long speech. It is clearly possible for listeners to extract information from a very weak voice signal, provided they are willing to expend the necessary effort. However, as the signal becomes weaker, the amount of effort required to decode the information carried by it becomes greater. Highly motivated listeners will expend considerable effort over a short period of time to decode messages that are sufficiently important to them; but as the speech grows longer, fatigue overtakes first the less motivated and eventually even the most highly motivated listeners. The effort required for further listening is no longer justified by the anticipated reward. Attention turns into easier channels and the audience member ceases to be an auditor; thereafter, except for sporadic trickles, the flow of information ceases. From this, we may formulate the following general principle: Information gain varies positively with the motivation of the listener, negatively with the extent to which the speaker's voice falls below a comfortable loudness level. Where motivation is high and the speech is short, even a weak voice, if intelligible, will probably result in maximum information gain; but where motivation is low or the speech is long, a weak voice will impair the transmission of information. Where motivation is low and the speech is long, information gain from a speech delivered in a weak voice may drop close to zero.

A second extraordinary condition under which the loudness of the voice can become important in information transmission is the presence of noise. Like fatigue, noise increases the amount of effort required to extract a given amount of information from a given signal. The greater the noise, the greater the motivation required to overcome it. The important variable in this respect, however, is not the absolute amount of noise present, but the signal-to-noise ratio: that is, the loudness of the noise relative to the speaker's voice. The human ear is extremely sensitive to sound; in fact, if it were only slightly more sensitive it would pick up vibrations produced by random collisions of air molecules. It is therefore not surprising that conditions of total quiet are almost impossible to obtain; there is always some noise, and in most speech situations there is a substantial amount. The speech signal, to be heard, must be louder at the listener's ear than the surrounding noise level: the louder it is relative to the background noise, the easier it will be to hear; and the weaker it is relative to the background noise the greater will be the amount of effort required to extract a given amount of information from it. Thus, loudness, noise, and motivation act together to help determine the amount of information gained by an audience. Where conditions are ordinarily quiet and motivation is high, any intelligible signal will probably result in satisfactory information gain; however, when the noise level is high or motivation low, a weak voice will result in a restricted flow of information to the listener.

A second variable known to affect the amount of information an audience gains from a speech is the rate of speaking. Estimates of the ideal speaking rate vary from 135 wpm to 165 wpm, but evidence indicates that listeners can absorb most kinds of spoken messages at a much faster rate.[4] Where the content of the speech is familiar and the style relatively easy (short words and sentences), auditors can listen comfortably and with full comprehension to rates in excess of 250 wpm, a value almost

[4]Grant Fairbanks, Newman Guttman, and Murray Miron, "Effects of Time Compression Upon the Comprehension of Connected Speech," *Journal of Speech and Hearing Disorders*, XXII (1957), 10–19.

never exceeded in even the most animated natural discourse. For instance, Walter Winchell's average gross rate was about 225 wpm, and even at his peak in the 1960 presidential campaign debates John F. Kennedy seldom exceeded 240 wpm, and then only for a few seconds at a time.

Evidence accumulated through many years of research on speech rate indicates that, insofar as communicating information is concerned, where the material is of no more than average difficulty the ordinary speaker need never worry about speaking too fast. In fact, since such information is absorbed as readily from rapid as from slow speech, he may actually communicate more information per unit of time by increasing his rate. However, when the speech is composed of material that is intrinsically difficult to understand, either in content or in style, rate may become a crucial consideration.[5] At this writing, most of the articles in such intellectual-appeal magazines as *Harper's* and *Atlantic Monthly* may be characterized as fairly difficult, and fall at about the level of difficulty at which rate comes into play as a consideration in information gain. The more difficult the material becomes above this level, the slower the rate must be in order to convey a given amount of information. In the McLuhan view mentioned in Chapter 2, "cold" material would require a slower rate.

Loudness and rate of speaking are known to affect the communication of information under certain conditions. All available research suggests that the influence of other variables of delivery upon information transmission is ordinarily slight, with the possible exception of speeches delivered under quite extreme conditions of noise, low motivation, or fatigue. For instance, pitch variation (or inflectional variety) is popularly thought to be extremely important in public speaking and its absence is thought to lower the communicativeness of a speech. Insofar as information transmission is concerned, the available

[5]Kenneth A. Harwood, "Listenability and Rate of Presentation," *Speech Monographs*, XXII (1955), 57–59.

evidence fails to support this conjecture.[6] Even a complete monotone apparently is not sufficient to impair the transmission of information in speeches of moderate length when audiences are reasonably motivated and distractions are minimized.

By the same token, the effects of vocal quality are quite negligible under satisfactory speaking conditions.[7] Where the speech is composed of intrinsically difficult material, certain extreme deviations from normal voice, such as would be considered pathological by speech clinicians, appear to impede the flow of information slightly; although not all pathological voice qualities have this effect. Oddly enough, the commonest voice defect seems to have the most deleterious effect: extreme nasality interferes with information transmission more than any other voice defect.

Slight though the direct influence of pitch variety and vocal quality upon the communication of information may be, it is probable that there exist conditions of high noise, low motivation, and great fatigue where differences in pitch and quality make significant differences in the amount of information gained by the audience. What appears even more likely on the basis of limited investigation is that these marginally effective variables may establish conditions in which the operation of the other variables is more pronounced. For instance, when the speaker's voice quality is poor, the negative effects of inadequate loudness may crop up sooner than when the speaker's voice quality is excellent; or, when the speaker's voice displays little inflectional variety, a slower rate may be required for the transmission of maximum information than when the voice displays great inflectional variety.

There is, then, no evidence to support the idea that loudness, rate, pitch variety, and vocal quality are invariably vital factors in the transmission of information in public speeches. On the

[6]Charles F. Diehl, Richard C. White, and Paul H. Satz, "Pitch Change and Comprehension," Speech Monographs, XXVIII (1961), 65–68.

[7]Charles F. Diehl and Eugene T. McDonald, "Effect of Voice Quality on Communication," Journal of Speech and Hearing Disorders, XXI (1956), 233–37.

contrary, under satisfactory public-speaking conditions most speakers are probably quite likely to produce speech that falls well within the tolerable limits of variation with respect to these aspects of delivery. Indeed, even extreme deviations from normal on any one variable seem to produce little if any harmful effect upon information transmission if all other conditions are adequate. Furthermore, it is erroneous to assume that mastering any one of the primary voice variables to perfection will greatly enhance a normal speaker's ability to transmit information effectively under normal conditions, since manipulation of either rate, pitch, quality, or loudness above intelligibility standards ordinarily has little effect on the audience's information gain. Wherever it has been possible to attribute a clearcut difference in information gain to one of these variables, the comparison has been between superior management of the variable and markedly inferior management of it.

On the other hand, when two or more delivery factors work together, or when extraneous factors such as fatigue, noise, or low motivation are introduced into the speaking situation, these variables of delivery operate like valves in the communication pipeline to restrict the flow of information.

VOCAL EMPHASIS.

In addition to their function as primary variables of delivery, the pitch, volume, duration (or rate) may be used by the speaker as devices to invite the audience's special attention to particular words, phrases, or ideas in the speech. Changing the pitch or loudness on a word or phrase, pausing just before or just after it, or delivering it at a slower or faster rate than the surrounding material is called "vocal emphasis." In their function as informational devices, these techniques are used in an effort to assure that the emphasized portions of the speech will be remembered more surely and more accurately than would otherwise be the case.

Though there are many different vocal emphasizers, they all

rely upon essentially the same principle: one or more of the delivery variables is temporarily altered during the utterance of the emphasized material so that it stands out by contrast from the context in which it appears. The rate is speeded up or slowed down, pitch is raised or lowered, pitch range is broadened or narrowed, volume is increased or decreased, stress is weakened or strengthened, or some combination of these techniques is employed.

Subjectively, vocal emphasis seems to contribute a great deal to the communicativeness of speech. Emphatic speech is impressive. Moreover, research supports the principal assumption underlying its use, for material that is emphasized in any of these ways is remembered better than other portions of the same speech.[8] However, vocal emphasis is not nearly so effective in this respect as purely verbal (linguistic) emphasis. For example, the simple expressions, "This is important" or "Now, get this," are roughly twice as effective as any known vocal emphasizer in assuring that audiences will recall a particular point. A simple repetition of the statement, either immediately or later in the speech, is considerably more effective than any method of vocal emphasis. While these examples show that vocal emphasis is not the only way, or even the best way, to assure transmission of a given bit of information, it is nevertheless true that the vocal emphasizers can make a significant difference in the auditor's memory of a specific point.[9]

This observation may lead the unwary to the conclusion that speeches with much vocal emphasis convey more information than speeches with little of it. That such is in fact not the case seems paradoxical, until one looks more closely at the function

[8]Charles H. Woolbert, "Effects of Various Modes of Public Reading," *Journal of Applied Psychology*, IV 1920), 162–85.

Ray Ehrensberger, "Effectiveness of Certain Forms of Emphasis in Public Speaking," *Speech Monographs*, XII (1945), 94—111.

[9]Arthur Jersild, "Modes of Emphasis in Public Speaking," *Journal of Applied Psychology*, XII (1928), 611–20.

of the emphasizer. Techniques of emphasis—vocal and other-wise—call attention to specific points; but in so doing they apparently draw attention away from points that are not emphasized. A passage delivered in an emphatic manner will indeed be remembered better than the surrounding passages; but the latter will, on the average, probably be remembered less well. The result will be the same total amount of information gained from the speech; the emphasis simply assures that certain points will be remembered at the expense of others.[10] When the vocal emphasis is such as to cause retention of the major or central ideas of the speech, then the emphasis is said to be effective. If, on the other hand, the pattern of vocal emphasis causes the listener to retain trivial and unrelated points, then the speaker is said to be guilty of misemphasis. If the speaker fails to employ any techniques of emphasis whatsoever, then the delivery of the speech will not exercise any control over which points the listener remembers, so that different combinations of significant and trivial points may be recalled more or less indiscriminately by one listener or another. Under these conditions, the speech will be said to lack emphasis, a criticism reflecting the expectation of most listeners that the speaker will supply them with cues as to which items in the speech are most important, and their corresponding annoyance when he fails to do so.

Let us take on a hypothetical experiment in public speaking. Two audiences, identical in all important respects, will hear the same speech. One audience will hear the speech delivered "effectively"; volume and rate will be adjusted to the topic and occasion, vocal variety, a good voice quality, and techniques of vocal emphasis will be employed. The other audience will hear the same speech delivered intelligibly but "ineffectively." How will the effects of the two speeches differ? If the speech is relatively short, the topic nontechnical, and the language simple, if there

[10]Grant Fairbanks, Newman Guttman, and Murray S. Miron, "Auditory Comprehension in Relation to Listening Rate and Selective Verbal Redundancy," *Journal of Speech and Hearing Disorders*, XXII (1957), 23–32.

is no excessive noise and the audience is highly motivated, there will probably be little if any difference in the amount of information gained by the two audiences. To whatever extent the above conditions are not met, the audience hearing the effectively delivered speech will gain more information than the one hearing the ineffectively delivered one.

Emotional Response

Because the emotions popularly are held to be favorite targets of oratorical charlatans and fakes (who in fact actually rely as much on specious argument as on emotional stimulation), the subject is treated frequently with suspicion and sometimes even contempt. It is nevertheless true that emotionality is frequently an important dimension of an auditor's total response to a speech, and on occasion it is the most important one. Emotional reaction may range from precisely what the speaker hopes the audience will "feel" to a response that is opposed to his purpose.

When a listener responds emotionally the response is most often associated with the ideational content of the speech; that is, the listener's emotions are aroused by images which the speaker's language provokes. To be sure, delivery alone is capable of arousing similar responses without the aid of any ideational content whatever, as shown by the oft-repeated story of Helena Modjeska. This famous Polish actress is said to have reduced an American audience to tears simply by reading numbers from a telephone book (in Polish) in heart-rendering tones with accompanying histrionics. Effects of this type are possible on the stage or on certain ceremonial speech occasions when the audience willingly suspends its beliefs for a short time in order to participate in a purely esthetic experience; but with the decline of ceremonial speaking the number of occasions upon which this type of response is possible has diminished markedly. Ordinarily the role of delivery in rousing the emo-

tions is less pronounced; it depends for its effect upon its interaction with the content of the speech.

According to one widely held view, the mechanism by which
the speaker adds emotional color to his ideas through management of the voice and bodily action is very straightforward. This
theory holds that certain vocal and visual cues are invariably
capable of arousing corresponding emotional states in listeners.
The speaker learns which stimuli trigger which responses and
then learns how to manage voice and body so as to produce
those cues deliberately. When he wants his audience to respond
with a given emotion, he emits the appropriate behavior which
produces stimuli that set off the corresponding emotion in the
listeners. If the listeners fail to respond in the desired fashion
then the speaker was not as skillful in delivery as he should have
been. This view has enjoyed a certain vogue among theoreti-
cians who consider themselves behaviorists, and such a "scientific" explanation in terms of specific stimuli and responses is
appealing to anyone who wants to reduce the stimulation of the
emotions to a technical skill. However, it is inconsistent both
with our present understanding of the emotions and with our
knowledge of how they spread from one person to another.

A basic flaw in the preceding theoretical formulation is the
assumption of a fixed number of specific and discriminable emotional states. The matter is not so simple. Emotional arousal is
associated with physiological changes, which may be highly
localized, but which tend to occur throughout the whole body.
Changes may occur in respiration, muscle tone, skin temperature, heart rate, blood pressure, digestive functions, blood chemistry, and the secretions of the adrenal, sweat, and tear glands,
as well as in other physiological functions. Any one of these
changes, or any combination of them, may be interpreted as an
emotional state, and since each physiological system may be
affected to greater or lesser degree on a given occasion, the number of possible arousal states is incomparably larger than any
list of "the emotions" could possibly represent. Certainly if such

a list existed, it would be so long that no speaker could reasonably expect to master the stimuli supposedly required to elicit all of the emotions.

The physiological changes that occur in emotion tend to be accompanied by patterns of muscular tension and activity. Changes in the large skeletal muscles influence the variables of posture and movement; contractions of the facial muscles influence facial expression; muscle tone is altered and the frequency, extensiveness, and rapidity of gesture are influenced. Not only are the superficial muscles affected, but the muscles of the vocal tract as well may become involved, altering the pitch, quality, and loudness of the voice, the duration of sounds, the depth and rate of breathing, and the manner of articulation.[11] As with the pattern of visceral and glandular changes, any or all of these muscular alterations may occur, to a greater or lesser degree. Unlike visceral and glandular changes, which are covert, these aspects of emotional arousal are visible and audible to others; they are the overt manifestations of the emotions.

Our present knowledge concerning the dynamic interplay between overt and covert aspects of emotional arousal is sketchy indeed; but, it is clear that the two tend to occur together and that any change effected in one tends to be accompanied by some change in the other. It is difficult to undergo the visceral changes of emotion without betraying them in the body and voice; too, actors report that a successful portrayal of an emotion usually requires that it be "felt" internally to some degree. A possible explanation of the actor's experience is that the behaviors characterizing an emotional state are so complex that any attempt to imitate them unfeelingly can be at best only partially successful, and a sufficient number of features is missing to spoil the performance. In public speaking the problem of

[11]Grant Fairbanks and Wilbert Pronovost, "An Experimental Study of the Pitch Characteristics of the Voice During the Expression of Emotions," *Speech Monographs*, VI (1939) 87–104.

imitation is ordinarily even greater than it is in acting, for the speaker does not have the benefit of the willing suspension of audience belief which is accorded the actor.

For this reason, the speaker who attempts to transmit to an audience an emotional state that he does not himself experience to some degree is faced with little prospect of success. As a matter of fact, most inexperienced speakers have some difficulty in conveying the emotions they do feel. The major cause of this difficulty is the feeling of inhibition which typifies early speaking experiences, and which depresses the more positive emotions the speaker might otherwise experience. Even when this feeling has passed, there remains a cautious reserve arising from a reluctance to express emotion publicly, a reluctance built up gradually through many years of social conditioning. To whatever extent this habitual reserve is operative, it will inhibit the visible and audible signs of the speaker's emotional arousal.

Despite these difficulties, it often happens that certain characteristics of the speaker's voice and action arouse in his listeners a feeling akin to what he is himself experiencing at the moment. This occurrence is perhaps best understood in terms of a process called "empathy." It is easiest to observe the occurrence of empathy in children watching a movie or television program. As they become involved in the action, they sometimes tend to imitate in miniature the movements and facial expressions of the actors. Whereas in children empathy sometimes takes this overt form, in adults the entire process occurs almost wholly in covert form. Small movements and changes in muscle tone show that the tendency toward imitation of the observed movement is present, though the overt imitation has been extinguished by years of conditioning. The fact that the muscular and the visceral components of emotional states tend to occur together may suggest the way in which empathy works. It has been suggested that minute muscular tensions occur in the listener as a sort of imitation of the movements of the speaker's superficial muscles and vocal tract; and these tensions tend to stimulate the visceral changes which have accompanied the imitated actions in the experience of the auditor.

The Speaker's Public Image

Listeners form impressions of speakers on the basis of whatever information is available to them. Obviously one source of information is reports of others—newspapers, acquaintances, and the person who introduces the speaker—concerning the speaker's character and abilities, experience, beliefs, and former actions. Another source of information is the speaker's connections and associations—the organizations he belongs to, the agency he represents, the people who are his friends and enemies. Secondhand and indirect evidence of this type helps to form a listener's general impression and expectations concerning the speaker before he begins to speak. During the speech itself the listener acquires additional information through what the speaker says. The sources of evidence he cites, the depth of experience he reveals, and the similarity of his attitudes and convictions to those of the auditor—all of which are revealed in the content of the speech—help the listener to shape an impression of the credibility and trustworthiness of the speaker and of his character and personality.

These, however, are not the only sources of information that the listener uses in building his image of the speaker; for throughout the speech the listener continuously modifies and reconstructs his impression of the speaker on the basis of the way in which the speaker talks. In fact, of all the effects of delivery the most pervasive and significant is its impact upon the audience's judgments of the speaker as a person. Small differences in delivery, which might have no appreciable effect upon the audience's retention of the information content of the speech or which might contribute but little to their emotional arousal, may produce a substantial difference in the image of the speaker, and through this avenue affect not only the short-run outcome of the speech but the prospects of the speaker and his potential effectiveness in future speeches.

Until recently, the concept of effectiveness in delivery has been associated primarily with efficiency in information transmission and secondarily with effectiveness in arousing emotion; consequently, little systematic work has been done with the role of delivery variables in determining the image of the speaker, even though evidence of their importance surrounds us on every side. Consider, for example, the careful attention paid to the combination of diction and intonation which we call "dialect." Network announcers on radio and television are ordinarily required to master a dialect with the misleading title "General American," which is the natural dialect of only a few native speakers. The reason often given for this is that regional or "substandard" dialects call attention to themselves and away from the content of the commercial. However, with the possible exception of extreme foreign accents there is no evidence that listeners gain significantly less information about the product from one dialect than from another. As a matter of fact, the principal advantage of General American as the dialect of broadcast advertising is that it leads the greatest number of listeners to develop a favorable image of the announcer and, through the announcer's increased credibility, to develop a favorable impression of the product he advertises.

We are far from a complete understanding of the operation of dialect in developing the image of the speaker, but its basic function seems clear enough. A speaker's dialect serves to categorize him in the mind of the listener. After hearing only a few words, most native Americans can identify speakers from the southern, the southwestern, the northeastern, and the midwestern states. Some can distinguish Virginia, Maine, and other state dialects. In most regions the dialect spoken in cities differs noticeably from that of small towns and farms. Residents of cities like New York, Chicago, and Pittsburgh, which were settled by numbers of different immigrant groups, can often distinguish among people from different parts of the city on the basis of their speech. Even the resident of an isolated community who may have heard only one dialect spoken during his entire life can readily identify any speaker as being "from here" or "from the outside."

Not only does dialect locate the speaker geographically, but it also locates him on a scale of status. In many communities, for example, the use of "ih" rather than "eh" in such words as "pen," "when," and "again" distinguishes low- from high-status speakers. In most places a clear articulation of certain final consonant sounds, such as the t's in "I don't want it," is perceived as a mark of the educated, influential minority. In fact, most of the rules of pronunciation and diction that are taught as "good speech" in the schools are indicators of social status; if followed, they tend to bring the student's speech behavior closer to what is perceived as the speech habits of the well-to-do, educated, influential (i.e., high-status) members of the community. Of all the goals that public education sets for itself, this is perhaps the hardest to achieve; consequently, with some exceptions, listeners can estimate the social status of a speaker with rough accuracy.[12]

In noting these effects of dialect upon the listener's image of the speaker, it is important to remember that, for the most part, they operate outside of awareness. That is, the listener is not aware of responding to specific characteristics of the speaker's dialect, but instead forms an immediate impression of the speaker's origin and class which, like our visual response to a tree or a dog, has the force and immediacy of a perceptual fact. We learn to distinguish a birch from an elm and a beagle from a collie long before we can identify the specific characteristics that separate one from the other and serve as the basis for discriminating between them. By the same token, most people

---

[12]L. Stanley Harms, "Listener Judgments of Status Cues in Speech," *Quarterly Journal of Speech*, XLVII (1961), 164–70.

cannot specify the individual speech traits that distinguish Dallas from Chicago and Quality Hill from the North End; they do not listen for individual speech traits and then consciously reason to a conclusion about the speaker. On the contrary, they form a total, immediate impression on the basis of the whole speech pattern which seems all the more real because it was not reached deliberately. Impressions formed in this way are quite resistant to change and exert a powerful influence upon thinking and behavior.

While dialect operates to locate a speaker geographically and socially, other characteristics of his speech contribute to the listener's evaluation of his personality and character. Of course, these impressions may be entirely wrong as first impressions often are; but they tend to be very clear impressions, most listeners tend to get similar impressions, and these impressions tend to exert considerable influence over the auditor's judgment of the speaker.[13]

Certain characteristics of delivery produce typical impressions in a wide range of listeners. For example, rate of speaking has been shown to exert a noticeable influence over the auditor's impression of the speaker's vitality. Rapid rates of speaking lead to an impression of activity, energy, and dynamism. Listeners view speakers who talk more slowly as if they were slower in other respects as well. Slow speakers are typically viewed as conservative, deliberate, or lethargic.

At least in our society, vocal pitch and loudness seem to be associated with the impression of strength. A low-pitched or loud voice is thought to characterize relatively strong personalities, whereas a high-pitched or weak voice is thought to characterize relatively weak ones. The fact that virtually everyone has personal acquaintances who belie this connection seems to have little effect upon the popular myth; initial impressions of speakers remain unaltered, and it may be only after extended

[13]Hadley Cantril and Gordon W. Allport, Chapter b, "Voice and Personality," *The Psychology of Radio* (New York: Harper & Row, Publishers, 1935), pp. 109–26.

contact with an individual that the impression of strength or weakness arising from pitch and loudness of his voice is finally overcome.

Listeners appear to respond to stress and the techniques of vocal emphasis as signs of assurance and conviction in the speaker. To most listeners, weak stress and unemphatic delivery lend an air of indefiniteness and indecisiveness to utterance. The speaker with emphatic delivery *seems* to know what he is talking about and to be convinced of the truth and importance of what he says. One of the qualities of the apparently confident or self-assured individual is that he habitually speaks in an emphatic manner.

Finally, the impression of liveliness, interest, and good cheer are associated in part with inflectional variety. The monotonous voice is characterized as lifeless, dull, or unhappy, and the individual whose voice displays these qualities is categorized in a similar fashion. When absence of inflectional variety is displayed in a single speech, the speaker is typically thought to be depressed or uninterested in the topic or the audience; the individual who *habitually* displays a narrow range of inflectional variation tends to be evaluated by others as a dull and cheerless person.

By this point it should be clear that this matching of vocal delivery characteristics with the personality evaluations of speakers could be extended indefinitely. The list is limited only by the number of adjectives we use to describe the personality traits of others; to each trait there likely corresponds a characteristic pattern of delivery to which listeners respond.

As we indicated earlier, the listener's categorization of the personality traits of the speaker on the basis of vocal cues frequently will be entirely false; but the important point here is not the validity of the judgment but the fact that it is made. Furthermore, like the response to dialect, audience response to these vocal cues occurs largely outside of awareness. The listener does not identify the basis of his opinion, he simply notes that the speaker seems energetic or deliberate, strong or weak, confident or unsure, lively or dull; and he is predisposed to respond to the speaker's message accordingly. Furthermore, since these factors generally operate on the margins of consciousness, their influence is stronger than they might be if the listener were fully aware of their operation. If the listener could verbalize the reasons for his judgment, such as, "This speaker sounds dull because his voice shows very little inflectional variation," he might perceive the flimsiness of the connection and reject the conclusion; but since he does not recognize the basis for his impression it seems to come to him as a stroke of insight and he is powerless to resist its influence.

It is of course obvious that vocal cues are not solely responsible for the image of the speaker. Though little is known about their influence, visible behaviors such as posture, gestures, facial expressions, and the like undoubtedly play a significant role. The age-old advice to stand tall, relax, gesture naturally, and look at the audience is designed to produce a pattern of visible behavior consistent with the image of a responsible, confident, sincere individual seeking to communicate directly with a group of listeners. For most speakers on most occasions the advice is undoubtedly sound, since this is precisely the impression that the speaker ordinarily wants the audience to obtain. We endorse this advice, though for somewhat different reasons than those often provided.

We have already indicated that delivery variables do not work alone to form the listener's impression of the speaker, but the foregoing paragraphs show that delivery plays a vital role in this process. Obviously any one of the connections between delivery and speaker image may fail to operate in the expected manner if there is overwhelming contrary information from other sources. For example, an extremely lively style of composition may offset a lack of vocal variety to such an extent that the speaker is perceived as an intrinsically interesting person in spite of what some would describe as dull and lifeless delivery.

Or, previous experiences with a speaker may have so damaged his credibility that what would ordinarily appear to be sincerity in delivery is perceived as a clever sham. We need to understand that discrepancies such as these do not constitute exceptions to the rule, but rather underscore an important point about the interaction of delivery variables with the other sources of information available to the listener.

Only very rarely will it be possible to trace to a single characteristic of delivery the cause of an auditor's impression of a speaker. The effects of rate, loudness, pitch, and dialect which we have discussed are clearly observable when they are varied one at a time, experimentally, with everything else held constant. In any natural speaking situation, however, these variables work in combination, and their effects are so intertwined that the influence of any one is difficult to detect. This is not to say that the influence of each variable is not present, but rather that the combinations of effects are more numerous and varied than a simple recital of the individual effects might suggest.

Not only is it generally impossible to trace the auditor's impression of the speaker to a single variable of delivery, but it is also impossible in most instances to account for the auditor's whole impression of the speaker on the basis of delivery alone, even when all delivery variables are taken into account. What others have said about the speaker, the groups with which he is associated, the sentiments he expresses, the values he implies, and the style of his language all combine with the variables of delivery to produce a single, more or less unified impression.

If the listener has at the beginning of the speech a great deal of information about the speaker, then the variables of delivery usually will do little more than help the listener to fill in missing parts of the personality picture. In doing so, he will tend to observe those things that are consistent with what he already knows and, unless the delivery departs radically from his expectations, will simply fail to observe any aspect of the speaker's delivery that conflicts with what he expected to hear. If he does notice it, he will ordinarily explain it away or minimize its importance. This, of course, is simply another example of the mental economy we all use to minimize the work of thinking by maintaining a harmonious balance among our attitudes, judgments, and impressions concerning a single object or person.

Thus, where the audience knows a good deal about the speaker before he begins to talk, the influence of delivery upon the speaker's credibility in a single speech will be negligible, unless the speaker is markedly poorer (or better) than the audience expected. When this occurs, the auditor is likely to reevaluate the validity of his previous information. It is for this reason that publicity agents occasionally advise their clients not to make public speeches, feeling that the client's bumbling, boobish style will destroy the favorable image that has been so carefully built up by mass media reports of his deeds. Most of us can remember being disappointed by at least one public figure when his speaking failed to measure up to the expectations we had formed on the basis of second-hand reports of him.

Despite the fact that such effects do occur, only rarely is a speaker's delivery so poor that it causes an audience to alter a well-formed favorable impression of him. On the contrary, delivery has its greatest impact on the image of the unknown speaker. Where the audience forms its initial judgment of the speaker from his speech, the variables of delivery play an extremely important role. Under these circumstances, delivery is noticed before the content of the speech has been sufficiently developed to provide a basis for judgment, and thus it is delivery that elicits the initial reactions to the speaker and sets tentative expectations concerning the speech. If the delivery is lively, assured, and direct, the initial impression of the speaker will be that he possesses these traits, and auditors will look for further evidence of them in the speech. Unless the content of the speech is notably at variance with this expectation, at the conclusion they will have formed a favorable impression of the speaker and will be more likely to view his ideas favorably than if his delivery pattern had created an unfavorable first impression.

Assignment: Analysis of Speakers

1. Attend a meeting where a significant public speech is going to be delivered by a speaker whom you have never heard before. During the first four or five minutes of the speech, try to estimate what judgments of the speaker's personality, character, competence, etc., will be made by most auditors of the type who are present at the meeting. During the remainder of the speech, analyze the speaker's voice and physical action to see whether you can determine what are the sources of these impressions in his speech delivery.

2. Attend a meeting or watch a television broadcast to hear a speech by a speaker whom you have seldom or never heard. Evaluate his or her performance on each of the secondary delivery variables. Does the speaker's delivery seem to enhance or inhibit effectiveness in terms of information gain, attitude change, or speaker image?

chapter 8

SPEECH AND

SOCIAL ACTION:

THE

IMPLEMENTATION

OF STRATEGY

Four of the eight chapters in this book (2, 5, 6, 8) deal particularly with the effect of social influences on public speaking. The final section on adoption and social action might serve equally well as introduction or summary to this set of ideas. It has been placed last because it contains both a group of considerations growing directly out of a specific speech situation and a more general set of concerns involving a number of messages over a period of time.

Because specific findings on the role of public speaking in the adoption process are limited, adoption models were not used as a framework on which to arrange all the other ideas on public speaking contained herein. But the authors do believe that the product of successful public speaking is adoption and have attempted to extend the relationship as far as data and logic will permit. Among other things, this final chapter reemphasizes the point that any particular speech is virtually always one of a number of messages on a subject coming to a respondent and that social action—or adoption—succeeds or fails because of (or perhaps in spite of) this flood of messages. The degree to which social influence may affect the immediate and subsequent reactions of an individual to a speech should also be carefully noted.

The investigation of how people adopt new ideas and practices has generated a considerable body of data and theory. This information has come from sociologists who have studied the adoption process among many groups, including farmers, physicians, educators, and industrial managers. The evolving theory of how people come to do things differently includes an attempt to define the stages of the process and to describe the characteristics of those who adopt early or late.

In any case, where the goal of public speaking consists either wholly or in part of getting people to utilize new ideas and practices, then we can make some use of adoption theory to develop a general view of public speaking in the process of social change. There are, of course, some important differences between attempting to change behavior through one speech delivered by one speaker to one audience and a campaign by many commercial representatives and agricultural agents during a nine-year period to get thousands of farmers to plant hybrid seed corn. Instead of discarding the comparison as grossly unequal, however, we should note that this large-scale, complex adoption was made up of countless small events involving interpersonal and mass communication. In fact, no effort in the "real" world involving bond issues, United Fund drives, college courses, religious instruction, or political campaigns is likely to be carried out exclusively by means of public speaking, and such an effort is never concentrated in a single, isolated speech. Rather, public speeches play a part in such programs, in company with many other communication events.

There is an unfortunate gap in the reports of adoption researchers concerning the role of public speaking. Adoption literature is without a specific mention of speeches in the process. This may reflect only a vagary in labeling; the broadcast medium is mentioned, and probably involves the transmission of some public speeches. It may also reflect limited perception in the investigators: public speaking may not have been found because it was not looked for.

But if adoption investigators seem to have ignored public speaking, it is equally true that many students of public speaking appear ignorant of, or indifferent to, the study of adoption. This is perhaps because compilations of adoption literature have been readily available only since about 1960. It may also be the case because theories of public speaking have focused often on the speech act almost as an end in itself, without much regard to predispositions, social context, and post-speech influences. Consequently, the experiences of change agents may not have been viewed as relevant to the task of the public speaker.

The fact is that studies of adoption represent one of the few systematic attempts to describe the role of communication in a program of social action. In discussing a strategy of oral communication, we have said in a variety of ways that a speech can be understood only in a broad social context which is present before, during, and after its delivery and that it is accompanied by a variety of other messages which both aid and hinder its acceptance. The heart of effective strategy as described in Chapter 2 is learning to adapt to these forces or to use them effectively. If we are to understand the role of communication in adoption, we should describe it in such a way that the presence and operation of public speaking are taken into account. First, therefore, we shall examine the adoption process in its own right; then we shall try to understand how public speaking plays a role in it.

THE ADOPTION PROCESS

One of the major concepts that investigators have isolated from their study of how people come to accept new ideas is labeled "the adoption process." Everett Rogers, one of the foremost investigators of adoption, describes it as the mental activity through which an individual passes from first hearing about an innovation to final acceptance.[1] As we mentioned earlier, adoption studies are usually based on units of time such as months or years, far in excess of the duration of a single speech. It is reasonable, however, to think of speech presentation and response as an adoption process in miniature, with acceptance or rejection occurring among individuals at various times during

[1]*Diffusion of Innovations* (New York: Free Press of Glencoe, Inc., 1962), p. 76.

and after the speech, and with audiences composed of early, middle, and late adopters who possess identifiable characteristics. From literature on the adoption process, we have extracted for discussion two ideas: the adoption period and the nature of individual adoption.

The Adoption Period

The adoption period is the length of time required for an individual to pass through the adoption process; that is, the interval between the time the individual first has made available to him information regarding a proposed change and the time he actually submits to or undergoes the change. In our mass-media-oriented society, it may seem unreasonable that individuals should have heard about a new idea or practice at widely differing times, yet in a study by Beal and Rogers concerning the adoption of a weed spray, some farmers reported hearing about the spray *seven years* before a number of others.[2] We can hardly assume that information about the spray in the form of stories and advertisements, broadcasts, contacts with agricultural agents and salesmen, and conversation with other farmers was delayed seven years in reaching some individuals. Rogers speculates that data must have been available to all at about the same time, but that only those who "wanted" to receive it selected the reports from their perceptual field. This process of "selective perception" in adoption has also been noted by Edward Hassinger.[3]

The adoption period is of particular interest to the public speaker/change agent because it suggests four concrete principles:

1. The success or failure of a particular speech depends in part on the speech; it also is related to whether the selective perception of some audience members causes the speech to be

[2]Rogers, *Diffusion of Innovations*, p. 109.
[3]"Stages in the Adoption Process," *Rural Sociology*, XXIV (1961), 52–53.

favorably received. If no one in the audience has had favorable past experience with a similar change, it is not likely that the speech will immediately produce change in anyone.

2. Care must be exercised in labeling a particular speech as a success or failure. A "successful" speech (that is, one that is followed by a high degree of adoption) may have occurred at a fortunate time in the life of the idea, when successful exposure to it has been experienced over a period of time. The apparent failure of a speech (when little or nothing results) may be in reality the beginning of exposure to an idea which will later enjoy a high degree of acceptance. Time and the amount of exposure, rather than the quality of a speech, may be the important variables.

3. The phenomenon known as "discontinuance" may further complicate any conclusion that a speech has succeeded or failed. Discontinuance is rejection of an innovation after it has been adopted. Audience members at a temperance lecture may rise and "take the pledge" at a meeting, but may not follow through on their commitment. Or they may abstain from drinking for only a brief time. Research into discontinuance supports the generalization that later adopters are more likely to discontinue than those who were among the first to adopt.

4. A successful social-action program will probably involve presentation of the ideas a number of times through as many media as possible. A preliminary education campaign may be necessary to prepare potential respondents before the key speeches are given. Well run United Fund campaigns and similar public appeals utilize this procedure to the fullest before a direct appeal is made for support. Apparently it is possible by means of a relatively brief message to precondition respondents either positively or negatively to later messages or events.[4]

---

[4]Irving Janis, Arthur Lumsdaine, and Arthur Gladstone, "Effects of Preparatory Communications on Reactions to a Subsequent New Event," *Public Opinion Quarterly*, XV (1951), 487–518.

The effect of such preconditioning is apparent even when the subsequent message or event proves to be different from what the preconditioning message would lead its recipients to expect.[5]

Paul Deutschmann's study of the 1960 Kennedy-Nixon television debates suggests the helpful nature of interpersonal communication in dealing with the barriers that selective perception may impose. Many persons learned of the debates and got information about them from friends, without having seen the debates themselves.[6] Selective perception is also more observable in interpersonal communication (for example in "live" public speaking) than in mass media. A speaker who is sensitive to feedback can detect selectivity in some respondents during the speech and make adaptations in his message or method of presentation in order to deal with it on the spot.

The Individual Adoption Process

Most investigators of farm practices have identified stages through which individuals pass in becoming adopters.[7] We can possibly utilize these stages as a model for what happens to a respondent when he reacts in ways intended by the speaker.

A. *Awareness Stage.* It is likely that an individual's initial exposure to a new idea or practice came from some print or broadcast medium. He is less likely to have heard about it from a personal source, such as conversation with a peer. Therefore, the public speaker should realize that he usually does not have the task of introducing a totally new idea to his audience. The stage has been set by some previous information received from

[5]Irving Janis and M. Hers, "The Influence of Preparatory Communications on Subsequent Reactions to Failure," in Carl Hovland, Irving Janis, and Harold Kelly, Communication and Persuasion (New Haven: Yale University Press, 1953), pp. 275–76.

[6]"Debate Viewing, Conversation, and Changes in Voting Intentions in Lansing, Michigan," (East Lansing: Communications Research Center, Michigan State University, 1961).

[7]Herbert F. Lionberger, Adoption of New Ideas and Practices (Ames: Iowa State University Press, 1960), pp. 21–32.

a relatively impersonal source. This is especially true for those respondents who are usually first in a group to adopt a new idea or practice.

B. *Interest Stage.* If a respondent becomes generally aware of a new idea and thus opens himself to receive more information about it, he is a candidate for the next phase in individual adoption—the interest stage. Although mass media continue to play an important source role, interpersonal sources now become significant as well. For early adopters, interpersonal communication from recognized specialists may be the most important, and it plays a larger role in the interest stage than do either mass media or conversation with peers. These findings indicate to the public speaker that he should rely on impersonal sources to introduce a topic and then should follow up with speeches to stimulate interest and supply information.

C. *Evaluation Stage.* Awareness and interest must be converted into a decision to adopt if the source is to succeed. The key factor here seems to be whether the proposed change is seen as relevant to the potential adopter's situation. At this point, farmers tend to turn to respected members of their own group for consultation. Conversation and group discussion are the most important interpersonal activities. Statements by individuals in specialized roles rank second. Specialists are more important to early than to late adopters. Speeches are important here, but the evidence does not suggest that public-speaking campaigns urging adoption of new practices will have as much effect as will reassurance from opinion leaders within the group. Therefore, a speaker should realize that even the best speech, presented at this stage, might not elicit immediate adoption; the respondent may require some time for cross-checking with peers to reinforce his tentative commitment.

D. *Trial Stage.* Not all new ideas and practices lend themselves to trial. The decision to buy a house, contribute to the United Fund, or vote for a candidate usually is a final commitment. Many other decisions, however, can be approached on a tentative basis. Conversion of a positive evaluation into a trial comes most frequently in connection with interpersonal communication with peers. Once a group has been judged ready to try out a new idea, public speaking can be of great importance in securing public commitment.

E. *Adoption Stage.* Research into the final phase—adoption—reveals that the experience of the potential adopters (which might be labeled intrapersonal communication) and the experiences of their peers are of greatest importance. Mass media and statements of specialists are used, not to aid in the adoption decision so much as to reinforce decisions already made and declared. This "confirming" behavior was discovered in the actions of new car buyers, who read ads about the cars they bought more than about cars they considered but did not buy. These selective tendencies were less pronounced among owners of older cars.[8] Of course, one of the goals of the change agent is to encourage the adopter to maintain his decision and avoid discontinuance. Therefore, speeches will be well-employed if they emphasize that the adopter is making a wise decision. Some situations may even call for postdecision persuasion to bolster and confirm commitments that respondents have already made.

One matter becomes clear as we study the nature of communication related to adoption. There is initially a source-receiver or speaker-respondent phase in which information is exchanged on a more or less one-person-to-one-person basis. There is also a time after the information has been presented when respondents turn to others for evaluation and reinforcement of what they have received. This phase, labeled the multi-stage flow of communication, will be considered next.

The Multi-Stage Flow of Communication

Traditionally, the public-speaking situation has been viewed as one in which the speaker exercised a prime effect on the in-

[8]D. Erlich, et al., "Postdecision Exposure to Relevant Information," *Journal of Abnormal and Social Psychology,* LV (1957), 98—102.

dividuals in the audience by what he said and did. Little additional attention was given to how the listeners modified one another's responses during and after the speech. When print and broadcast media began to be studied, this same "one-way" model was employed. The influence of the mass media was seen in terms of a newspaper or radio broadcast which communicated directly with the individual reader or listener. In studying the influence of mass media on voting behavior in the 1940 presidential elections, Paul Lazarsfeld and associates found that information flows not only from media to "consumers," but also from those persons through interpersonal channels to less informed sectors of the population.[9]

Rogers hypothesizes that the first step, from source to opinion leaders, consists mostly of a transfer of information; the step from opinion leaders to others involves the spread of "influence."[10] Although it is unquestionably an interesting attempt to analyze the differences between these stages, this view may overlook the credibility of the original sources and the conditions under which the message was first presented. It seems more likely that influence, in the sense of favorable connotation, begins with the original source and continues through the process.

The two-step idea was an important breakthrough in thinking about how communication flows. More recent research suggests a multi-step situation in which the process of receiving and passing on to others is repeated a number of times, so that for a considerable period after its original release, the message is broadly diffused through interpersonal communication. We can, then, view each member of an audience as a potential retransmitter of the ideas presented in the speech, and each of his contacts as a potential reretransmitter.

A study of association patterns among people confirmed the existence of "opinion leaders" who influenced clusters of people

[9]*The People's Choice.* New York: Columbia University Press, 1948.

[10]Rogers, *Diffusion of Innovations,* pp. 213f.

around them. In general, these opinion leaders seem much like the people they influence. They do not maintain their leader roles on all subjects, but may defer to other persons on some matters. Interpersonal relations thus serve both as communication networks and as sources of social pressure and support.[11]

The multi-stage flow hypothesis has been ignored by investigators in the field of public speaking, and little research is available to indicate whether the same process operates in the speaker-audience relationship. Research done on the hypothesis comes from the sociology of mass communication and from studies of adoption. Since mass media often report or transmit public speeches, the idea seems relevant. We can speculate that the effect of a speech will begin at the time the speech is given or somewhat before and extend for an indefinite period afterward, while it is being discussed by those who heard it and described by them to people who did not. While a speech is in progress, the respondents will begin to tell one another about their reactions through cheers, applause, cat-calls, yawns, or silence. Some will also exchange whispered comments. When the speech is over, the exchange will be more extensive as respondents gain physical access to other audience members.

Just how influential is this overt response by audience members? In one study of the effect, under experimental conditions, a recorded speech was presented that contained statements contrary to the previously tested norms of the audience. Applause for some of these statements was also present on the recording. Some audiences in the study were told that the original listeners were different from themselves; other groups were told that the audience on the recording was similar to themselves. The "similar" audiences tended to exercise a more favorable influence on the listeners than "dissimilar" audiences. So whether cheers or boos influence an individual may depend on

[11]Elihu Katz, "The Two-Step Flow of Communication: an Up-to-Date Report on an Hypothesis," *Public Opinion Quarterly*, XXI (1957), 61–78.

whether he perceives the noise as coming from persons with whom he can identify.[12]

We should not assume that this multi-stage transmission activity is uniform for all persons who are present at a speech or who later hear about it. Those who are directly interested and concerned with the content of the message are far more likely both to receive and to pass on comments than are those who are only marginally involved or indifferent. This factor of involvement has been tested by Leon Festinger and others.[13]

When comments are made among audience members after a speech they will generally be directed toward three goals:

1. *To Verify.* "Now, as I understood it, the speaker said that . . . ." Here the questioner attempts to reinforce his impressions by stating them to another, often a person whom he respects. By doing this, he invokes the possibility that his original perceptions may be challenged or modified, as well as reinforced.

2. *To Supplement.* "I didn't get that second main point . . . ." Respondents are seldom able to recall completely the development of a speech, particularly a longer speech such as a lecture or sermon. If the speech has captured their attention, they attempt to fill in blank spaces in their recall by questioning others. Once again, the possibility of variation in the original message is introduced.

3. *To Evaluate.* "That was quite a speech, but . . . ." Perhaps the most frequent and also most potent comments are those that make judgments about the over-all effect, or about the speaker's delivery, choice of ideas, or organization of material. Evaluative comments are usually of a highly voluntary nature and may be made to anyone who has shared the experience of hearing the

[12]H. H. Kelley and C. L. Woodruff, "Member Reactions to Apparent Group Approval of a Counternorm Communication," *Journal of Abnormal and Social Psychology,* LII (1956), 67–74.

[13]"A Study of Rumor: Its Origin and Spread," *Human Relations,* I (1948), 464–85.

speech. While a politeness bias operates in some evaluative comments ("Fine speech, wasn't it?" "Yes, wasn't it.") such remarks are usually highly predictable and ritualistic and probably exert little influence. Comments involving sincere praise or rejection are usually more detailed.

The second stage of communication, consisting of such exchanges as these, is likely to determine in part what the respondent remembers after some time has gone by. If we label the statements the speaker has made as Speech X, the speech that the respondent recalls before he discusses it with anyone may be Speech X, or X_1, or something quite different. Second-stage comments, then, may have the effect of moving the respondent closer to, or further from, Speech X. We should certainly note in this connection that the important speech often is not the one the speaker made, but what a majority of the audience thought he said. While the second-stage interaction is going on and after it has been completed, the respondent will probably be serving as a primary source for others who did not hear the original speech. Thus the pattern of influence may be repeated in a multi-stage fashion. There is some evidence that when persons have heard a speech contrary to their beliefs, they will seek out persons who agree with them, and that this discussion may tend to "blank out" the original content of the speech.[14]

We have presented a view of the public speaker partially at the mercy of a web of social influence. This may seem at considerable variance with the legend of the orator-giants of the past who held audiences within their control. Many attempts have been made by speech critics to explain the power of these speakers in terms of style, potency of ideas, or compelling delivery. Another view that merits consideration is that orators such as Webster, Clay, Douglas, and Bryan had an understanding of how to utilize social influence to achieve positive reinforcement of their views. They may have been timely diffusers

[14]May Brodbeck, "The Role of Small Groups in Mediating the Effects of Propaganda," *Journal of Abnormal and Social Psychology*, L (1956), 166–70.

in the adoption process. Whatever the reasons for the success of these men, we know that the speaker in the mid-twentieth century operates in a somewhat different environment. His audience is literate, mobile, and saturated with information and opinion from the mass media. What can he do to utilize the multi-stage flow of communication in ways favorable to his goal and to counteract possible diluting and distorting effects of the multi-stage process? Research in the area has not provided us with many useful answers. We can, however, gain some insight by observing practices that seem to work. Some of these are:

1. *Provide advance information about the topic and viewpoint.* By using appropriate techniques to let the potential respondents know what the speech will be about, the speaker can reduce time spent by the audience in "tuning in" on the speech. National leaders and other prominent figures often release the text of a speech to the press in advance of its delivery. One of the effects of this practice is to provide extensive orientation to the speech through mass media coverage, as well as to provide an accurate printed record of what was said. Not every public speaker is important enough to receive such attention, but similar ways are often available. The college teacher who takes a few minutes at the end of his lecture to describe what will happen during the next lecture is attempting to accomplish much the same thing. Clubs and organizations frequently have newsletters which can carry orienting material about upcoming speeches. Posters, advertisements, and notices can also be used for orientation. When a speaker is to be formally introduced, the chairman can provide some "warm-up" material about the subject.

2. *Build feedback devices into the speech.* A speech will generate in the respondents the desire to communicate to others about it. If the speech has a "closed" format—and some situations, such as sermons, sharply restrict feedback—then nearly all second-stage comment will occur after the speech, when the direct control exerted by the speaker has been removed. The most fre-

quently employed device is the question-and-answer technique. It has the merit of requiring little preparation. Among its limitations is the fact that it is highly personalized and may meet the needs of only a small number of respondents while wasting the time of those not interested in the matter. It is also subject to politeness bias, in that respondents may ask about only socially acceptable matters, or may ask questions to meet the speaker's expectations that questions be asked. One interesting specialization of the question-and-answer device used in communication training programs is labeled the "information conference." This may be employed in situations where understanding is crucial. The speaker solicits questions and then waits. He brushes aside or answers briefly all queries that appear to be asked merely to meet his expectations. After a waiting period of several minutes, which tends to generate a high degree of tension in those present, questions may appear that indicate a basic misunderstanding or disagreement not previously apparent. Whether the matter can be cleared up depends, of course, on many factors, including the nature of the problem and the skill and willingness of speaker and respondent. At least the discussion will occur under conditions where the speaker can exert some control over it.

Another feedback device that may be used, if time and conditions permit, is the "buzz session." After introducing some ideas, the speaker gives the respondents a task, such as a question to be answered or a situation to be analyzed. He divides them into groups of about six persons and gives them from six to ten minutes to reach conclusions. Then he may call for one report per group or may solicit individual responses that have been stimulated by the discussion. Once again, this enables a portion of the initial verifying, supplementary, and evaluative comments to take place under somewhat controlled conditions. The opportunity is present for the speaker to respond to misunderstandings and objections which may have been verbalized during the buzz session.

3. *Provide reinforcing visual cues in connection with the speech.* If the speaker is reasonably confident that he will not deviate extensively from his planned message, he may distribute outlines of the speech. He may also provide pictures, cartoons, and charts as a means of reinforcing what he says. If the visual aids really have a reinforcing effect, they will reduce partial recall or distortion following the speech and make the reaction more favorable by increasing clarity.

But repetitions of a message, at least in a single form, seem to have diminishing returns. In one study of student behavior, a student population was divided into three experimental groups and a control group. One group got a single leaflet that was against the subsidization of athletes. A second group received a different leaflet each week for three weeks. The third group got a different leaflet each week for five weeks. A post-test of attitudes toward athletic subsidization was conducted on all the students in the study. The single leaflet produced a significant decline in favorable attitude toward subsidization. The three leaflets produced a stronger effect than one, but not significantly so. The effect of five leaflets, however, was no different from that of the single message.[15]

4. *If possible, arrange to have the main ideas from the speech repeated in some form following the speech.* Many political and religious speakers distribute copies of their remarks. Reports by sympathetic mass media accomplish the same thing. So do references to the speech by other speakers and writers with a similar viewpoint. Such reinforcement may appear at important stages in the communication flow.

SUMMARY

The process of adopting new ideas and practices provides a valuable model to the public speaker in making decisions about

[15]R. W. Dietsch and Herbert Gurnee, "Cumulative Effect of a Series of Campaign Leaflets," *Journal of Applied Psychology,* XXXII (1948), 189—94.

how he should proceed. Success and failure of a speech should be judged relative to the passage of time, rather than to events that occur immediately after the speech is given.

The physical delivery of a speech is a vital part of oral communication, but it does not describe the total event. The second stage, during which audience members verify or supplement their recollections of the speech and exchange opinions about it, also contributes extensively to how the respondents finally perceive it. Although the speaker cannot control these events, he may be able to introduce factors that will increase the probability that multiple stages of communication will operate in ways favorable to him.

Assignment: Adoption Within an Audience

In a given speech audience, there are likely to be persons who correspond to the classes of adopters described in the discussion of the adoption process (early, middle, and late adopters). In your next speech how will you anticipate and attempt to control this phenomenon?

Control of Multi-Stage Transmission

Assuming that one of your speeches this term is a "real" speech to a "real" audience, describe orally or in writing how you plan to use the suggestions in Chapter 8 concerning control of multi-stage communication flow.

INDEX

A

Abstraction, 70, 71, 82, 86
Accuracy, 48–50
Action of body during speech, 157–58
Activation level of audience, 114, 117
Adoption of New Ideas and Practices, 188n
Adoption process (new ideas), 183–90
Allport, *see* Cantril and Allport
American Medical Association, 50
Analogies, 22
Analysis:
    of audience, 105–45, 190–97
    of content, 76–80, 82–83
Anecdotal support, 78
Aristotle, 18
Articulation, 151
"Attention material," 98–99
Attitudes, 22–25, 118
Audiences:
    activation level of, 114, 117
    analysis of, 105–45, 190–97
    as receivers of speech, 12–14, 28, 30–35, 83–84
Authoritative support, 78
    see also Credibility

B

Beal, *see* Rogers
Bell Telephone Laboratories, 18
Berleson, *see* Waples and Berleson
Berlo, David K., 19, 19n
Bloom, Benjamin, 21n, 23n
Bodily action (during speech), 157–60
Brehm (J. W.) and Lipsher (D.), 45n
Brodbeck, May, 194n
Brookings Institution, 51
Broom, *see* Merton, Broom, and Cottrell
Bruner, Jerome S., 34–35, 35n
Bryant (Donald C.) and Wallace (Karl R.), 105n
Bryson, Lyman, 18n

"Buzz session," 196

C

Cantril (Hadley) and Allport (Gordon W.), 175n
Carmichael (L.), Roberts (S. O.), and Wessell (N. Y.), 159n
Change agents, 6–9, 40, 42–45, 53
Channels (sensory), 19, 149
Code, 29
Communication:
    effectiveness of, 85, 104, 117, 120, 124–25, 139, 160–80, 186–90
    models and theory, 17–19,
    as a purpose of the speech, 4–5, 28, 107, 116
The Communication of Ideas, 18n
Communication and Persuasion, 188n
Composition, *see* Structure
The Conceptual Framework of Public Communication, 52n
Conclusion, 98–99
    see also Form
Connotation, 24, 191
Constraints in choice of content, 112, 119–21
Content, 15–17, 46–48
    criteria of, 111–12, 119–21
    in terms of purpose, 28–29, 31–33
    see also Structure
Context (of elements in the speech), 58–69, 72–73, 77–78, 83–85
    see also Social context
Cooper (Joseph B.) and Michiels (Lawrence J.), 25n
Cooper, Lane, 18n
Cottrell, *see* Merton, Broom, and Cottrell
Coules, *see* Thibaut and Coules
Credibility, 47–48, 50–51, 172, 173, 178–79, 191
Criteria of content, 111–12, 119–21
Crutchfield, Richard, 32, 32n